This Boo...

Extra LIVING

What Happens When God Works Through You

Dear Mary Jones,
Thank you for being for Christ. You are an extraordinary woman!
Love,
Andrea
Ephesians 1:17-19

By Andrea Jones Mullins

Finished Reading thru 3/29/02

Extraordinary LIVING

What Happens When God Works Through You

By Andrea Jones Mullins

New Hope® Publishers
Birmingham, Alabama

New Hope Publishers
P. O. Box 12065
Birmingham, AL 35202-2065
www.newhopepubl.com

Library of Congress Cataloging-in-Publication Data

Mullins, Andrea Jones, 1948-
   Extraordinary living! what happens when God works through you / by
Andrea Jones Mullins.
      p. cm.
Includes bibliographical references.
   ISBN 1-56309-525-4 (hardcover)
   1. Christian life. I. Title.
   BV4501.3 .M85 2001
   248.4--dc21

                              00-012054

Unless otherwise noted, Scripture quotations are from the *New Revised Standard Version of the
Bible*, Copyright © 1989 by the Division of Christian Education of the National Council of the
Churches of Christ in the USA. Used by permission. All rights reserved.
      Verses marked TLB are taken from *The Living Bible*, Copyright © 1971 by Tyndale House
Publishers, Wheaton IL. Used by permission.
      Scriptures marked NASB are taken from the NEW AMERICAN STANDARD BIBLE ®,
© Copyright The Lockman Foundation 1960, 1962, 1963, 1968, 1971, 1972, 1973, 1975, 1977.
Used by permission.
      Scripture taken from *The Message*. Copyright© by Eugene H. Peterson, 1993, 1994, 1995.
Used by permission of NavPress Publishing Group.

All uncredited poetry is the original work of Andrea Jones Mullins.
Cover and book design by Cheryl Totty
Cover photo by Karim Shamsi-Basha

ISBN: 1-56309-525-4
N014111 • 0401 • 7.5M1

ॐ Dedication

To my family
  For this journey we have taken together,
  For reminding me of what is most important,
  For being Christ to me,
  For the love and support that has meant so much,
  For laughter and tears shared,
  And for living life abundantly!

To Mike, for always.

In memory of
  Pat and Bill, my brothers-in-law, whose generosity
  and friendship I miss,
  and
  my father, who believed in me and anticipated the
  writing of this book.

ॐ Table of Contents

But we have this treasure in clay jars, so that it may be made clear that this extraordinary power belongs to God and does not come from us.

—2 Corinthians 4:7

❧ Introduction

God is the subject of this book. God is extraordinary. *You* are the object—you are an ordinary person with an extra-ordinary God. The message is simple. The extraordinary God gives ordinary people extraordinary lives.

I know from experience that God takes ordinary people and gives them extraordinary lives. When I consider what God has done for me, I know that He can do anything with anyone. Fortunately for us, extraordinary living is something God does. God is not limited by what we have to offer. He looks at our lives through the lenses of divine grace. While we are asking, "What does God want me to do?" He is waiting for us to ask, "What has God done for me?" *The Message* gives us this interpretation of Romans 12:1: "So here is what I want you to do, God helping you: Take your ordinary, everyday life—your sleeping, eating, going-to-work, and walking-around life—and place it before God as an offering. Embracing what God does for you is the best thing you can do for him." Extraordinary living is God's work.

God offers extraordinary living to those whose lives are all that they had hoped it might be. For instance, my friend Edna is celebrating the birth of her first grandchild and writing a sequel to her book on mentoring. My niece Rachel has just started her dream career after completing a challenging state exam. My friend Karry is building a home with her beloved husband Mark. A co-worker has just returned from an anticipated prayer journey in Bosnia. With positive experiences such as these, we can easily believe that life can be extraordinary.

God's offer of extraordinary living is also available for those whose days are overflowing with schedules and responsibilities. My daughter Michele is the mother of three young children. She serves as room mother, takes her children to tap and soccer and swimming and day camps and reading clubs and field trips and church and doctors and. . . . Get the picture? Even busy schedules can't keep us from God's wonderful offer.

Most amazing of all is that God offers extraordinary living to those who face crises and chaos, like my friend who has both parents in her home, one with Alzheimer's and one with another serious illness. Another friend's husband has been unemployed for months; she is working in a job she doesn't like, and she is dealing with an undeserved legal battle. Other friends are dealing with issues such as a painful divorce, a sick spouse, personal illness, and a recurring sense of failure. Pain and crises cannot keep us from the extraordinary life God can give. He is well aware of our triumphs and of our tears. He knows when we are taking "the wings of the morning" as well as when we are making our "bed in Sheol." I am convinced that extraordinary living is not situational, for it is something God does.

What if you have already gone for years without accepting God's offer of extraordinary life? What then? Don't give up! I remember Lulu, an outstanding businesswoman and winner of several awards, who turned 65 with an empty heart. Years of living apart from God's plan had made her suspicious of anyone who mentioned *love*. When a group of women in the community invited her to meet with them each week in a Bible study, she joined them out of loneliness. She often told the group that they were not to say the word *love* to her because she did not believe in it. Lulu watched these women. She saw how they lived and how they cared for her and for others. She read the words of the Bible with a new understanding of God's love for her. Finally, she could resist God's love no longer and gave her life over to His care through His Son Jesus Christ. She discovered that God's love for her was so great that He loved her just as she was, with a lifetime of weaknesses, failures, and wrong decisions. She discovered extraordinary living.

At the same time, God is doing the extraordinary all around us and invites us to join Him in accomplishing His purposes for our world. As you read *Extraordinary Living!* you will find three sections. Section One is *Prepare for an Extraordinary Life*. My goal for this section is that you will discover how God is equipping you for an extraordinary life. Section Two is *Look for the Extraordinary Work of God*. God is at work and He wants you to know what He is doing. The extraordinary life is found in the places where God is at work. Section Three is *Live the Extraordinary*. Living life to the fullest depends on some basic tools. Both chapters focus on essential tools for extraordinary living.

Preparing, seeing, and living are simultaneous and cyclical. God is preparing us while at the same time we are seeing His work and joining Him in what He is doing. The more we see His work and join Him, the more He is able to prepare us. The more we are prepared, the more He will show us and the more He will involve us in His mission.

I invite you to join me in a journey of discovery. Why has God created you? What has God done for you? These are the questions that we will answer together. My desire is that you know and experience all of the life that God has planned for you. My prayer is that your life will encourage others to discover for themselves the abundant life—extraordinary living.

❧ Where Extraordinary Living Begins

Extraordinary living is found in a personal relationship with God through His Son, Jesus Christ. Jesus came to bring abundant life to all who trust in His name. Abundant life comes when you confess that you are not living as God intended and you accept the forgiveness that is yours in Jesus Christ.

Jesus is God's Son. He lived on earth to show us who God is and how God wants us to live. Although Jesus lived a perfect life, those who hated God crucified Him on a cross. When Jesus died, He paid the price for your failure to please God—your sin.

Jesus conquered sin by dying on the cross. He conquered death by rising from the grave and He lives now at the right hand of God in heaven. When you trust Him with your life, He comes and lives within you through God's Spirit, the Holy Spirit. You will have abundant life now and for all eternity.

The Bible says in Ephesians 1:7–8, "In him we have redemption through his blood, the forgiveness of our trespasses, according to the riches of his grace that he lavished on us." Because of Jesus you are forgiven for your sin!

Extraordinary living begins in this commitment of your life to God. If you have not trusted Christ with your life, sincerely pray this simple prayer or your own prayer. God will hear! *Dear God, I have lived in disobedience to the way that You would have me live. I do not want to live that way any longer. I ask Your forgiveness. I believe that Your Son Jesus died for me. I want the abundant life that You offer. Help me to know You and to know that You love me and forgive me. Amen.*

When you pray in sincerity, God comes into your life and makes you into a new person. Through Jesus Christ you become a child of God. I urge you to trust Him now so you can join me in discovering how God gives ordinary people extraordinary lives.

Chapter One

Extraordinary Living Is God's Plan

Missing the mark and losing my way,
So little to offer, so little to say,
His offer of love, of forgiveness, of place,
The offer of heaven, abundance of grace,
All that is needed, His for the giving,
To an ordinary woman—extraordinary living!

The bus stopped at a busy corner in Moscow. My friends and I gathered our bags of Russian New Testaments and stepped out on the sidewalk. The rain was beating down hard and dripping off the edges of my umbrella. I juggled the umbrella and the bag, trying to keep from getting too wet, while watching for someone with whom I could talk. Through the rain, I saw a tall young man beside me. "Minya zavoot Andrea," I said. He smiled. "Ya Americana," I said. He smiled. "Ya Christiana," I continued. He smiled. I pulled out my Russian language guide to read the phrase I had worked so hard to learn. "I want to give you a Bible," I said. He smiled. I repeated the phrase. "You want to give me a Bible?" he asked—in English! We both began to laugh at my poor Russian language skills.

Then I asked, "Have you ever read the Bible?" "No, I've never seen the Bible," he responded. I opened a Russian New Testament to John 3:16 and pointed to it. "Can you tell me what this sentence says in English?" Standing in the rain, the young man slowly translated the verse from Russian into English with my help. And so it was that a young man named Andrea (same name as mine) heard of God's love for him. A few moments later, He gave his heart and life to Jesus as Savior and Lord.

I handed Andrea the Russian New Testament. "I am taking this Bible home. I will read it to my wife and little girl. I want them to know Jesus, too," he said. Andrea reached into the sack he was carrying and pulled out something wrapped in newspaper. He handed the small package to me, and I unwrapped a beautiful crystal bowl he had just purchased on his way home. Although I protested, I could not turn it down when he said, "Take this with you to America as a gift for telling me about Jesus and to remind you to pray for me, my family, and my country."

Extraordinary living. Whatever you think that means, you had better get ready for something far greater. The experience on a Moscow street corner is only a glimpse of the beyond-belief life that God provides.

❧ The Motivation for Extraordinary Living

Did you catch the last two words in the paragraph you just read? *God provides.* Extraordinary living is what God does. Living life has a whole new motivation and energy when we put our focus on God, not on ourselves. God's mercies, God's goodness, *God helping us* is what gets us up in the morning looking toward the possibilities with an attitude of expectancy, a mindset of hope. Now our motivation is the goodness of God. We know that all good things come from God. His plans are for our good, and His mercies are the only worthwhile motivation for us to give ourselves completely over to God's plans.

When you get up in the morning, forget about looking in that mirror to see if you have what it takes to get through the day successfully. I can tell you right now that you do not. Praise be to God because He *does* have what you need in order to live victoriously, taking hold of the grand journey laid out before you. "Therefore, my beloved, just as you have always obeyed me, not only in my presence, but much more now in my absence, work out your own salvation with fear and trembling; for it is God who is at work in you, enabling you both to will and to work for his good pleasure" (Phil. 2:12–13).

This passage should end with one giant exclamation point! God is working in our lives. He is mercifully protecting us, leading us, and empowering us for each new day and each new opportunity. What a freedom we have in realizing that the extraordinary life we are looking for is what God does for us. Extraordinary living is not anything we have to do for ourselves.

❧ The Ignition Point for Extraordinary Living

God wants to give you an extraordinary life, and He tells you exactly how to accept this life He gives. Look at Romans 12:1. Notice the operative phrase "present your bodies as a living sacrifice." Turning your life over to God is the ignition point for the extraordinary life. Take a break from reading and do something for me. No, do it for yourself. Go into your kitchen and find a large bowl or briefcase. Walk through your house gathering items that represent every aspect of who you are—photos, calendars, business cards, keys. When you have your bowl or briefcase full of items that are aliases of your life, symbolically offer them to God. As far as I can tell, I can trust no one else as much as I can trust God with all the parts of my life. What about you?

Sadly, many of us never quite grasp this fact of faith. We keep working ourselves into a frenzy of emotion, frustration, and anger. We are disappointed that we have not done something we thought we should have done or become someone we thought we should have been. Love, joy, peace, patience, kindness, gentleness, faithfulness, goodness, and self-control are right there for the taking; but we live as if we are satisfied with so much less. We behave as though extraordinary living is something reserved for a select few—or for no one.

❧ Extraordinary Living Is the Solution to Life's Puzzles

Life experiences can leave us wondering if God can change lives. When my neighbor's brother was found tortured and murdered, I never dreamed that the murderer would be someone I know, someone I saw fairly often, someone popular in the community. The murderer carried his hatred until the very end of his life. He believed murder would solve life's puzzle, but his actions only brought further grief.

Even in my own life, no matter how much I try to get life's letters to spell the right words, the puzzle goes unsolved. This is similar to my crossword-puzzle ability. By the time I complete one, any confidence I had in my vocabulary is totally destroyed. I now keep the solution page at hand so I can fill in the words I don't know. I like having the answers right where I can see them! Life would certainly be easier if I had a solution page to turn to.

Actually, life does have a solution page, available to every individual. The solution is *in Christ*. In Christ, the doors of heaven are opened and all the blessings of God are lavished on us. "It's in Christ that you find out who you are and what you are living for" (Eph.1, *The Message*). Life is a puzzle, but God knows what the finished picture looks like. He alone understands the puzzle of your life and where each piece fits. My sixteen-month-old grandson and I were sitting on the floor playing with a wooden puzzle of animal shapes. Nicolas was trying to put a lion-shaped puzzle piece into a chicken-shaped hole. He tried over and over to get that lion piece to fit into the chicken space. Do you think it ever went in? Of course not. As Nicolas gets older, if he continues to try to get a lion to fit into a chicken, his patience will turn into frustration and anger. On the other hand, I knew where the puzzle piece would fit. When Nicolas let me guide his hand to the right place, the puzzle piece easily slid into place.

Don't you and I try to do the same thing with our lives? The Father has the pieces of our lives in His hands, but we think we know better than He does where they go. So we take them out of God's hands and try to make the puzzle of our lives a complete picture. We take the lion-shaped pieces and force them into chicken-shaped holes, and we wonder why we aren't whole. We live without a sense of direction or design. The idea of an extraordinary life is crazy for people who are just a bunch of pieces without purpose.

What if I told you that you could let God have the pieces of the puzzle of your life back? What if I told you that extraordinary living is at the other end of the spectrum from sleeping through life? What if I told you that there is a solution to your life, that God has it, and that He is offering it to you? What if I told you that God's solution will give you an extraordinary life? Do you believe this is possible? I had to accept this reality for myself, and so must you.

ટ Five Realities of Extraordinary Living

1. God has an extraordinary plan for ordinary people.

Karry did not have the advantage of a Christian home, but God had a plan for her life. She decided as a young girl to choose God's plan. Today, after graduating from college and seminary, she has a fulfilling ministry, is married to the man of her dreams, is building her first home, and is looking forward to every opportunity for service that God sends her way.

The prophet Jeremiah communicated God's intention for the lives of His people: "For surely I know the plans I have for you, says the Lord, plans for your welfare and not for harm, to give you a future with hope" (Jer. 29:11). The writer of Psalms experienced the right hand of God upon his life and gave us a metaphor describing the intimate involvement of God in our daily lives: "In your book were written all the days that were formed for me, when none of them as yet existed" (Psalm 139:16).

Scripture makes it clear that God's plan for your life is intentional, not random. God did not wait to see who your parents would be before deciding what to do with your life. God did not leave your being born to chance. There are no accidental lives. Even a beginner's knowledge of God confirms the intentional plan of the Creator. God *intends* something for your life.

One of the most significant events of my life was the day I realized that my life had purpose. I had been in and out of church for a few years when I realized that I was celebrating Christmas without any visible evidence that I knew who Jesus was. In the living room of my home, I made a new commitment to seek God's plan for my life. A few months later, I moved with my husband and daughter to a small town in Wyoming where I began to grow in my understanding of God's plan for me.

The small church in our community had a women's group that met each week. Most of the women were like I was; we were young mothers, immature in our faith. Also in the group were several godly women who taught us the value of prayer and Bible study. As I began to include God in my daily activities, He began to change my understanding of personal identity and purpose for living. One day I realized that every part of my life, even *cleaning my house*, was of value to God, part of God's plan for me. I am not an exceptional housekeeper, but I have a changed attitude toward housework since that time. Work I had never wanted to do suddenly became enjoyable! I was doing this for God. This was His work.

A few years ago I was in a weekly evangelism group with three other women. Our goal was to increase our effectiveness in sharing our faith through our various lifestyles. One of the women worked in a high-stress vocation. She disliked her workplace and had hard feelings toward some of her co-workers. Her prayer was that God would take her out of the situation and give her a new place to work. We prayed with her, but God worked in a different way. She began to see her workplace in a different light. What had been a trap became a place of ministry. Co-workers saw a change in her attitude and behavior. She discovered other Christians working with her, and they began to walk and pray together. Co-workers came to her for advice and found Christ as well. She realized that being in that particular workplace was not an accident but an intentional action in God's extraordinary plan for her life.

During a women's conference where I was speaking, I heard a missionary share how she was trained for a specific type of ministry. When she arrived on the mission field she was given the one assignment she had absolutely no desire to do. At first, she was angry and prayed to be released. During her prayers one day she became aware of the incredible opportunities she was having as a result of this unwanted ministry assignment. From that moment on, she was filled with love for her assignment and later found turning the assignment over to another person hard.

She discovered that her ministry was not a random accident, but an intentional plan of God for which He had been preparing her for years.

Whatever you are doing—cleaning your home, driving in a car pool, caring for a sick child or a homebound adult, working in a stressful job, trying to make ends meet, using your skills to meet a need—is valuable because God is working out His plan for you!

Living with this sense of intentionality is one of the most incredible factors that separates the Christian lifestyle from any other lifestyle. This is why Paul could say with absolute confidence, "For to me, living is Christ and dying is gain." Paul knew that every event and experience of his life had eternal significance. If he was in prison or if someone took his life, God's plan for Paul would be fulfilled. We may think that prison and persecution that leads to death would hinder what God wanted to do in Paul's life, but not so. Nothing about Paul's life was random. Nothing about your life is random. God has a plan as important and exciting as Paul's, and your plan is designed just for you.

2. God has prepared an extraordinary ministry for ordinary people to do.

"For we are what he has made us, created in Christ Jesus for good works, which God prepared beforehand to be our way of life." (Eph. 2:10)

Chariots of Fire is an inspirational movie about the Olympic athlete Eric Liddell. Eric was a Scottish runner on Great Britain's team in the 1924 Olympic Games. God had called him to the mission field, but Liddell also felt God had called him to run. A scene in the movie portrays Liddell explaining to his sister why he has to continue to run in the Olympics. He tells her, "When I run, I feel His pleasure."

Liddell understood that God prepared him to do ministry not only as a missionary, but also as a runner. In real life, Liddell made headlines when he refused to run on Sunday at the Olympics. His witness touched many hearts, including those of his fellow athletes. His Christian commitment resulted in his running the 400 meters in which he won the gold medal. While Liddell did not realize that he would be making headlines because of his call to ministry, he did know that his running was for a specific purpose of ministering as God provided opportunity. He used his international fame as a runner to teach others about Christ.

When I renewed my commitment to God and became active in a church, I recalled that I enjoyed singing. The desire to sing returned, and I finally had the courage to give it a try. I gave my voice to God and He blessed me. An important part of my ministry is singing, and when I sing, "I feel His pleasure." I believe that God created me in Christ Jesus to sing, and when I sing He is pleased. I also believe that I do other things that please God because they are the *good works* that He prepared in me for His purpose.

You were remade in Jesus for good works. Good works are impossible without God, because good works have eternal purpose, the intentionality that only God can give. Before God, without God, your way of life was a complete contrast to the life of good works that God planned for you. While all of us appreciate good deeds done by anyone, the value of works done apart from God do not measure up against the good works that come as a result of the intention of God *in Christ*. Hopefully, this book will enlighten you even further about what your doing "good works" means.

Note some important things about good works. First, *good works are God's plan*. He has already decided what you are to be about in life. The guessing game is not of God. He wants you to know His plan. If you are open to hearing from Him, He will let you "feel His pleasure."

Second, *good works are God's doing*. His power and His character make good works possible. When we begin to think that good works are something that we do rather than God's doing *through* us, we fear our inability to live up to God's plan. We lose the power of God that turns a work into a *good* work. Rejoice with me. God will do good works through you. That is His plan.

3. God leads ordinary people into an extraordinary life of service.

"For the Son of Man came not to be served but to serve, and to give his life a ransom for many." (Mark 10:45)

"So if I, your Lord and Teacher, have washed your feet, you also ought to wash one another's feet." (John 13:14)

I started a conversation with a woman seated next to me on a plane going to Orlando, Florida. She had taken a short vacation from her work. Or should I say her ministry? She started her own cleaning business, primarily cleaning homes. You may think, "nothing about that sounds extraordinary." The extraordinary came in her sense of call, of purpose, of joy, and of love. Her goal for each home she cleaned was that the family who lived there would sense the presence of God because she had been there cleaning and praying. Her plan was to bring people into the kingdom through the quality of her work and the spiritual value she added to the physical labor each time she cleaned. She felt God's pleasure when she cleaned. She knew her life had eternal significance, and life was an exciting daily adventure. She loved serving.

God set the example. He came to us in an attitude of service. I find it hard to get my mind around the fact that the Lord of Lords, King of Kings, the Great I AM came to serve us. I have imagined Jesus kneeling at my feet with a towel and a bowl of water, gently taking my foot in His hand and washing it. He looks at me and smiles with such love that my heart is broken. The only option I have is to fall on my face before Him and confess my unworthiness of such love. Service calls forth that kind of response. No wonder Peter cried, "Lord, not my feet only, but also my hands and my head."

What a difference it makes in my day when I commit myself to serving my family, my fellow workers, and the persons that I encounter in my daily routines! I come out of myself and find a joy and fulfillment that is missing when I focus on getting my personal needs met and having my way. I am freed from the bondage of jealousy, envy, pride, greed, and covetousness when I serve. Do you think that God knew this would happen when we serve? Could it be that He called us to serve because He knows serving will free us from bondage and fill us with joy?

4. God can use every ordinary skill, talent, ability, and experience in extraordinary ways.

"Like good stewards of the manifold grace of God, serve one another with whatever gift each of you has received." (1 Peter 4:10)

"We know that all things work together for good for those who love God, who are called according to his purpose." (Rom. 8:28)

First, *God is eternal*. He is not limited by time. He is not locked into the temporal. Second, *God is all knowing*. Human beings are locked in time and know only a small part of any situation or person. I have lived with my husband for more than 30 years, yet I still know so little about him. His thoughts are hidden from me. I am with him only part of the time and have only second-hand knowledge of his life when we are separated. Even when we are together, I am limited in my ability to understand where his attitudes come from or what he feels at any given moment.

God, on the other hand, looks at us from the perspective of our entire beings. He sees us from before the time we were born and throughout eternity. He is intimately aware of our every thought and every action. He knows exactly why we behave in certain ways, and He knows what we will do before we have even thought it. God's ability to know us so completely allows Him to take everything about us and turn it toward His purposes. God wants to use us for the good works He has planned. A nice smile, a loaf of homemade bread, a talent of sewing, the ability to weld, patience to sit with the sick, the gift of gab, a green thumb, an hour-long drive to work, a failed marriage, an organized mom of six or a laid back mom of three, a follower or a leader—all are within the bounds of God's good plan for your life. Are you getting the picture yet? God can and will use everything about you to give you the abundant life. Get ready to see what God can do with what may seem valueless to you.

5. God calls us from mundane, ordinary, boring, tedious lives to extraordinary living.

"This signet from God is the first installment on what's coming, a reminder that we'll get everything God has planned for us, a praising and glorious life" (Eph.1:14).

Miss Irene was more than 100 years old. She lived across the street from my parents. She lived alone, was hard of hearing, and had very little vision. She couldn't read or watch television. She had outlived almost all her dearest family and friends. Even so, to be around her was to be around the Son. Her joy encouraged all who visited her. She even cooked for you—if you were courageous enough to eat it! She claimed the glorious and praising life and was living it to the end. Have you met people who seem to glow from within, even though their lives are difficult at best? Continuous praise for God's goodness is on their lips. We must each remember that even in times of difficulty, God's very Spirit is at work bringing us glorious lives.

Life lived in Christ, for Christ, and through Christ is as far removed from boring as Mt. Everest from the Everglades. Nothing about God and His people is boring. The life God planned for you will not take you around the same short track day after day after day. His plan includes a new song every day. His plan is dynamic, fulfilling, and inspirational. Some thought the apostle Paul was trapped on a short track going round and round while he was in prison, but Paul found his bondage to be a gift from God. You do not have to leave the place where you are. Nothing has to change except your desire to accept God's gift. The life God offers is not dependent on external factors. Wherever the Holy Spirit is indwelling God's child, that is the place where God is working out the abundant life.

God knows that life is hard and that we need continuous reminding of His plan for us. My extended family has experienced violence, crime, abuse, divorce, unemployment, financial loss, serious illness, death. Life seems hard to me. Life is so hard, in fact, that if it were not for the Holy Spirit prompting us to look beyond the evils of this world to see God's hand in our lives, we would miss out completely. We would forget to even consider that life can be extraordinary!

The Holy Spirit reminds you and me every day that God offers better than the life this world offers. We are offered the praising and glorious life already planned for us. Grab it. Hold on to it. God wants you to have it right now!

Chapter Two

What I've Learned About Extraordinary Living

Living is Christ
Loving is life
Giving is privilege
Going is right
Doing is service
Purpose is call
Power is God
Hope is for all

The spectacular view of Lake Louise in Canada is a distant second when compared with the glimpses of Christ we see each day. The Swiss Alps and the Wyoming Tetons pale when measured against moments when we awaken to a new reality of our faith or when we see another life redeemed from destruction. The turquoise waters of the Caribbean coast pale when set against the comfort of God given through a friend or the grace of forgiveness received from one we have injured.

The Bible story of Paul and Silas singing in the prison always interests me. How could two believers be so joyful in such a desperate situation? I wonder at Joseph who walked victoriously through trial after trial. How could he be so positive when he was hated, abandoned, sold, falsely accused, and imprisoned? How could biblical heroines, missionaries, and martyrs through the ages live with anticipation of the next hour and the next day regardless of their life situations? I now know that extraordinary living is a reality and it is not dependent upon our life situations. What an awesome truth!

At times I thought my life had to be perfect to experience the extraordinary life God offers. I had to be brighter and wiser. I had to work harder and act like others who seem to have it all together, or start all over. Then I discovered that extraordinary life is right there, mine for the taking! Right there in the midst of family struggles, professional stress, disappointments, physical weariness, and a multitude of other hindrances, I can experience the extraordinary life. What in your life makes you think you cannot experience God's offer of extraordinary life?

Financial problems?

Rejection?

Illness?

Depression?

Care giving?

Death of a loved one?

Loneliness?

Divorce?

Marital problems?

Parenting failures?

Something else?

Reading this list makes me want to throw back my head and laugh with abandon. None of these factors keeps God from giving us an extraordinary life. He is bigger than any of these. Only our unwillingness to take Him up on His offer can keep us from this marvelous gift. Are you ready to take God's extended hand and go with Him into life?

Aztec, New Mexico, is the place where I first realized that God was reaching for my hand. I was a little girl attending Bible study. My teacher saw in me a desire to know the Jesus of whom she spoke. She took me aside and introduced me to Jesus Christ as my personal Savior. I remember the morning I was baptized. Just before I went under the water, I looked out to see my mother in the congregation.

At that time, my father was not a Christian. My mother was the one who took my sister and me to church. From the time we were young, she kept us involved in Bible schools. Since we moved a number of times in my childhood years, I am especially thankful for her efforts and her understanding of the value of faith and a church family. As I grew up, I remembered the commitment I made in Aztec, and I had an awareness that I belonged to God. When I look back, I can see that regardless of how often we moved, God never lost sight of me.

My eighth-grade year is a spiritual marker along my faith journey. While we were living in Louisiana that year, my father went out of town to a meeting. On his way home, he heard a Christian radio broadcast. The message was aimed at my father's heart, and he gave his life to Christ. He changed in many ways. Even in my sometimes-turbulent teen years, I could see Christ in my father. His heart for evangelism and ever-forgiving spirit was a significant influence throughout my adult years as I made decisions about my ongoing commitment to Christ.

When I reached young adulthood, I decided to go my own way for a season. I know I wounded the heart of God and others in my family with some of the decisions that I made. Surprisingly, even as I wandered in a dark land, I knew that God had a special plan for my life. At one time I told my husband that I felt God calling me to ministry. God had not lost sight of me.

Mike and I had been married for about four years when I could resist the loving arms of Christ no longer. A few times in my life, I have heard God's voice so clearly that I felt like I had almost heard Him audibly. This was one of those times. God came down to me. His voice broke through my apathy. He knew that buried within my heart was a longing for Him that could not be satisfied apart from living for Him.

Even standing alone in my home I felt my face flush with the awareness of my sinfulness. Many times through the years I have been grateful that we have a God who knows the truth about us, but those were the times when I had been wrongfully accused. This time was different. I was guilty and God knew it. I knew it. I yearned for His forgiveness and cleansing, which He poured out on me with love that would not let me go.

Once again my heart was awakened to God's call, and a new hunger for spiritual things began to grow. Not long afterward, Mike and I moved from one state to another. Our new home was a small community in the southwest corner of Wyoming on the edge of the Uinta Mountains. I've sometimes compared the Christian community I found there with the protected environment of Palestine, the place where the Lord led Israel to prepare them as His chosen people. I believe one reason that God specifically led us to this community was to strengthen our relationship with Him.

What a change my heart experienced as I saw the heart of God lived through our pastor, his wife, and my fellow Christians! I began to understand that God gives ordinary people extraordinary lives. Every day brought new opportunities to see what God would do. From that day to this, life has not failed to be extraordinary. When I am open to receiving and participating in the life that God offers, the possibilities for abundant living are boundless. I know from experience that ordinary people can live extraordinary lives.

Experience is only one reason that I believe in extraordinary living. Above all else, I believe the Bible confirms that God's plan for each of us is extraordinary. Consider a few of the verses that speak to God's plan for those who love Him. This is His offer of extraordinary living.

God is doing an extraordinary new thing: "I am about to do a new thing; now it springs forth, do you not perceive it? I will make a way in the wilderness and rivers in the desert. The wild animals will honor me, the jackals and the ostriches; for I give water in the wilderness, rivers in the desert, to give drink to my chosen people, the people whom I formed for myself so that they might declare my praise."—Isaiah 43:19–21

God is giving extraordinary strength: "Those who wait for the Lord shall renew their strength, they shall mount up with wings like eagles, they shall run and not be weary, they shall walk and not faint."—Isaiah 40:31

God is performing extraordinary healing and restoring: "Then the eyes of the blind shall be opened, and the ears of the deaf unstopped; then the lame shall leap like a deer, and the tongue of the speechless sing for joy. And the ransomed of the Lord shall return, and come to Zion with singing; everlasting joy shall be upon their heads; they shall obtain joy and gladness, and sorrow and sighing shall flee away."—Isaiah 35:5–6,10

God is doing extraordinary things in our lives: "With joy you will draw water from the wells of salvation. And you will say in that day: Give thanks to the Lord, call on his name; make known his deeds among the nations; proclaim that his name is exalted."—Isaiah 12:3–4

God is giving extraordinary protection: "The Lord is your keeper; the Lord is your shade at your right hand. The sun shall not strike you by day, nor the moon by night. The Lord will keep you from all evil; he will keep your life. The Lord will keep your going out and your coming in from this time on and forevermore."—Psalm 121:5–7

God's extraordinary life is for all our years: "The righteous flourish like the palm tree, and grow like a cedar in Lebanon. They are planted in the house of the Lord; they flourish in the courts of our God. In old age they still produce fruit; they are always green and full of sap, showing that the Lord is upright; he's my rock, and there is no unrighteousness in him."—Psalm 92:12–15

God has given us an extraordinary place in His great mission: "But you are a chosen race, a royal priesthood, a holy nation, God's own people, in order that you may proclaim the mighty acts of him who called you out of darkness in to his marvelous light. Once you were not a people, but now you are God's people; once you had not received mercy, but now you have received mercy."—1 Peter 2:9–10

Do you know of any other god, any corporation, any organization, any person on earth, or any other religion that offers the life promised to us by the Lord our God? Do the Scriptures above describe an ordinary existence or an extraordinary encounter with a living God who fills us with Himself so that we might join Him in His extraordinary plan for the ages?

I encourage you to do your own Scripture search to decide for yourself whether God's plan for you is ordinary or extraordinary. The Bible is filled with verses of Scripture that reveal the extraordinary plans of our God for His ordinary people.

🕊 I'm Still Learning What It Means to Live Extraordinarily

Tonight I got caught in a traffic jam beside a woman who intentionally made a right turn from the left-hand lane because she didn't want to wait behind three cars to turn. I went to pick up conference programs from a printer only to find that they were still not ready although they were due two days earlier. I got home to find that the books I ordered had still not arrived. They were to have been here two days before, too. I expressed my dissatisfaction to the printing company, complained to myself about the traffic, and refused to give way to the "lane trespasser." Other than that, I was my normal gracious self.

As you can see, I am still learning what it means for God to give an ordinary woman an extraordinary life. For a few minutes out there in the traffic I actually came to my senses long enough to spend time in prayer for my family. It was wonderfully relaxing. I even forgot that my car was not moving. I do not understand how I can so quickly forget how soothing the prayer was, but I soon returned to my mental madness. I'm afraid to chart the percentage of time I spent in prayer against the amount of time I spent in frustration.

Extraordinary life calls me back to the reality of what being human is really all about. I mean being human in the way that Jesus was human. Out in the traffic, I caught a glimpse of the extraordinary life when I let go of my frustrations and filled my mind with prayer. For a few minutes, I was living in peace, joy, hope, and fulfillment. The aggravations of life were completely overcome by God's activity in my heart. If I had stayed my mind on God, I would have gone home with an outlook that brought a smile to another face or hope to another weary traveler, all evidence of living in the extraordinary.

Jesus is the example of extraordinary life. He was human in an extraordinary way. "What would Jesus do?" has been a popular question in the last few years. If Jesus had been in the traffic, His mind would have focused upon the peoples' needs. He never missed seeing a hurting and neglected soul. If Jesus had found the conference programs still unfinished, He would have realized that the person He was speaking with was not the one responsible. He would have had compassion as the situation was explained. If Jesus had encountered the woman making a right-hand turn from the left-hand lane, He would have given way in an attitude of service and humility.

Living and responding to the world as Jesus would is the direct result of living in complete obedience to the Father. Jesus had no secret power or knowledge that helped Him live differently from the way I live. The very power and knowledge Jesus had is also available to me. The Father will give me as much as I am willing to receive. Jesus was willing and capable of receiving all that the Father had to give, for He communed with the Father 100 percent of the time.

Jesus did not hide His formula for obedience. He shared it with His followers so we could also know how to live in obedience to the Father.

"Very truly, I tell you, the Son can do nothing on his own, but only what he sees the Father doing; for whatever the Father does, the Son does likewise."—John 5:19

"When you have lifted up the Son of Man, then you will realize that I am he, and that I do nothing on my own, but I speak these things as the Father instructed me. And the one who sent me is with me; he has not left me alone, for I always do what is pleasing to him."—John 8:28–29

Can we see what the Father is doing in the same way that Jesus did? Yes, the more we communicate with Him through prayer, the more alert we will be to His work in our lives and in our world. I cannot join Him in His activity until I see where He is and what He wants done. Jesus was perfectly in tune with God; He was always aware of what the Father wanted Him to be and to do. Consider for a moment what Jesus has done in order for us to know and experience the joy of doing God's will.

- Jesus has made it possible for each of us to have an intimate relationship with the Father. "I am the way, and the truth, and the life. No one comes to the Father except through me. If you know me, you will know my Father also. From now on you do know him and have seen him" (John 14:6–7).
- Jesus is our advocate so we can live in the extraordinary. "My little children, I am writing these things to you so that you may not sin. But if anyone does sin, we have an advocate with the Father, Jesus Christ the righteous; and he is the atoning sacrifice for our sins, and not for ours only but also for the sins of the whole world" (1 John 2:1–2).
- Jesus confirmed the Father's love for us and prayed for us that our joy would be complete. "For the Father himself loves you, because you have loved me and have believed that I came from God" (John 16:27).
- Jesus came so that we could have life abundantly. "I came that they may have life, and have it abundantly" (John 10:10).

Tomorrow I will have another opportunity at the same corner when I turn to go home. I will be back at the printer, and I will talk again to the company who shipped my books. I want another glimpse of the extraordinary life as I go through these ordinary tasks. Will you join me in learning to live in the extraordinary?

&. *I Do Not Always Feel Extraordinary*

The house has not been cleaned well for several weeks. I haven't been able to fill an empty staff position that has been vacant for almost a year. I need to write several thank-you notes and call some friends. I'm debating with myself about the vacation days I had planned to take with my daughter and her family in a few weeks. Some projects that should be tucked away with the word *completed* are still hanging over my head. Today I slept two hours later than usual. Now I feel more behind. The flowers I nurtured all summer completely wilted yesterday when I forgot to water them and the temperatures reached 100 degrees Fahrenheit. The food selection in the pantry is pretty bleak unless you are happy with cereal for every meal.

These are the everyday experiences that keep me from feeling extraordinary. Many women experience more serious situations that can keep the feeling of extraordinary an unrealized reality. In the foreword of *A Woman of Excellence* by L. Jane Mohline, Dr. Gary Collins writes about the traumatic issues women face.

"Many women don't feel praiseworthy. Every day thousands face the trauma and indignity of abuse, violence, and harassment. Many carry the pain of childhood rejection, molestation, and failure. Some are treated as second-class citizens by church leaders who should know better. No estimate could predict how many struggle with poor self-concepts, insecurity, depression, and loneliness—sometimes brought on by the thoughtless words and actions of insensitive and self-centered men.

"Jane Mohline knows about these rejections and insecurities, because she struggled with them for most of her life. Despite the gentle and sensitive support of a caring husband, she had come to view the excellence in Proverbs 31 as an ideal that few (if any) ever come close to reaching. Most of the women she knew were like herself: 'females who struggle with problems.'"

Jane writes that she struggled with guilt, depression, and inadequacy throughout her life. She tells of women who faced serious life issues and how they found their way to a new understanding of womanhood. Jane's book affirms the truth that we do not always feel extraordinary, especially when life's issues overwhelm us.

For many years, I did not realize that life could be extraordinary. I didn't wake up to God's intention for life. Situations like the ones I described at the beginning of this section would have caused frustration and cynicism. Simple daily issues cause our esteem and our understanding of our personal value to God and His plan to flounder and falter. We do not feel extraordinary, and few persons could convince us otherwise.

Feelings are powerful forces. My particular personality is stronger on feeling than on thinking. That means that I prefer to feel my way through a situation rather than think through the facts. Actually, my intense feelings can blind me to the facts. If I feel ordinary, then I refuse to see the reality of the extraordinary. Fortunately, God knows that feelings are often hindrances to the reality of what He offers us. The apostle Paul wrote of the Lord's faithfulness regardless of our feelings. Read aloud with me Romans 8:38–39.

"For I am convinced that neither death, nor life, nor angels, nor rulers, nor things present, nor things to come, nor powers, nor height, nor depth, nor anything else in all creation, will be able to separate us from the love of God in Christ Jesus our Lord."

Paul felt insignificant, unworthy, and defeated. He knew pressure to perform and to excel. He was aware that his feelings could make him doubt God's power for his situation. I do not know Paul's personality type, but I do see a man of passionate feelings. His letters flow from intense feelings rather than from a methodical and analytical approach.

Extraordinary living is not based on feelings. If you are like me and need help thinking through your feelings, try the following techniques by Norman Vincent Peale. These suggestions focus on the role of thinking in overcoming adversity.

1. Organize a mental attack on your troubles by organizing your thought and bringing order to the situation in your mind.
2. "Prayerize" your adversity by allowing God to show you how He can help you.
3. Change your thinking to see any and all of the advantages you may have because of the adversity.
4. Trust your ability to think so you can remain calm in waiting and anticipating God's guidance.
5. Let God be the source of your thoughts for He is the greatest thinker of all time. "No set of adversities can stand up for very long against the individual who draws upon God's thinking."

The extraordinary life God offers is better than any feelings you might have. The Lord does not give extraordinary life based on your feelings, but rather on His steadfast love. He doesn't give up on you or withhold from you anything that will make your life a blessing.

❧ When I meet Elijah, I will be able to say, "I understand where you were coming from!"

What a great day it was! God came down at the perfect time to light a fire and destroy the testimony of the prophets of Baal. Elijah was riding high. The people repented and the false prophets were destroyed. Elijah was proven by the Lord Himself to be the true prophet of God.

The story is a made-for-TV drama. While 450 prophets marched around their prepared sacrifice, calling on Baal to light the fire underneath, Elijah taunted them with the inadequacy of their god. "Cry aloud! Surely he is a god; either he is meditating, or he has wandered away, or he is on a journey, or perhaps he is asleep and must be awakened" (1 Kings 18:27). In their frustration, the prophets began to mutilate their own bodies in an effort to get their god to respond, but all to no avail.

The prophets were humiliated, but that was just the beginning. Now was Elijah's time to call upon his God. Elijah repaired God's altar with twelve stones. On the stones, he laid a pile of wood; and on the wood, he placed the bull to be sacrificed. Around this Elijah built a trench. He soaked both the bull and the wood on the altar with twelve jars of water, filling the trench with water as well. Following this preparation, Elijah prayed.

"O Lord, God of Abraham, Isaac, and Israel, let it be known this day that you are God in Israel, that I am your servant, and that I have done all these things at your bidding. Answer me, O Lord, answer me, so that this people may know that you, O Lord, are God, and that you have turned their hearts back" (1 Kings 18:36–37).

The Lord did not leave Elijah and the people wondering which God was the one true God. The answer came swiftly and strongly, leaving no doubt.

"Then the fire of the Lord fell and consumed the burnt offering, the wood, the stones, and the dust, and even licked up the water that was in the trench. When all the people saw it, they fell on their faces and said, 'The Lord indeed is God; the Lord indeed is God.'" (1 Kings 18:38–39).

The people were so deeply convicted of their sin that Elijah had their complete cooperation in seizing and destroying the 450 prophets of Baal.

Not many of us have had such powerfully visible evidence that we are God's chosen instrument. Few people have been in situations where they were so obviously the victors over their enemies or had such a large audience for their successes. I cannot imagine a more vivid assurance of God's power and faithfulness. How could Elijah ever doubt God again? Yet only eight verses later, the Scriptures tell us something surprising after such a mountaintop experience. "Then he was afraid; he got up and fled for his life, and came to Beer-sheba, which belongs to Judah; he left his servant there. But he himself went a day's journey into the wilderness, and came and sat down under a solitary broom tree. He asked that he might die: 'It is enough; now, O Lord, take away my life, for I am no better than my ancestors' " (1 Kings 19:3–4). Elijah left a mountaintop experience only to turn and run from Jezebel in fear. His fear was so great that he asked God to take his life.

I do not know how discouragement can set in so quickly, but I know that it does. Sometimes when I am enjoying the events of a moment, a song or a word reminds me of my father's death. I experience a sudden sensation of deep gloom and loss, and the tears start to flow. Even as I recall the wonderful times that I had with him, I am also overwhelmed with sadness and a longing to see him again.

Life is, and can be, both fulfilling and frustrating all at the same time. God is proving Himself faithful in one area of our lives while we are running our own show in another. Then the two collide. Sometimes this collision can bring on some serious physical and emotional ailments. For Elijah, the collision meant depression.

Elijah did not immediately recover from his depression. First, he sat in the wilderness under a lone tree. The Lord sent an angel who fed him and sent him to a cave. When Elijah was somewhat physically restored, the Lord asked, "What are you doing here, Elijah?" Elijah's depression still gripped his heart as he responded to the Lord. "I have been very zealous for the Lord, the God of hosts; for the Israelites have forsaken your covenant, thrown down your altars, and killed your prophets with the sword. I alone am left, and they are seeking my life, to take it away" (1 Kings 19:10).

Only days before, God had proven for all of Israel that He alone is sovereign and that He is indeed Lord. Elijah could not see beyond the difficulty of the moment. Does God wonder at mankind's inability to remember His goodness? Does the Lord marvel that He could do so much for us and yet it is never enough?

A few years ago my pastor preached from Psalm 42. His topic was how to deal with difficult times. One point of the sermon and of the Scripture passage is the importance of remembering. "These things I remember . . ." are the psalmist's words as he recalls the wonderful times he has had with the Lord. The question the psalmist asks is *why*, in light of these wonderful memories of God's faithfulness, *is his soul still discouraged*.

I have asked this very question of myself. When I struggled with an important decision, I found myself becoming quite depressed. Depression was something I seldom had felt. I could not overcome my self-centeredness enough to change the situation. A friend suggested a simple cure. She encouraged me to end each day listing the ways that God had been good to me, giving thanks for each of His kindnesses. The first night was difficult as I tried to see beyond my discouragement, but I was determined to try. Each night I quietly spoke thanks for each good thing of the day. My last thoughts before sleep would be of God and His goodness.

When a person begins to see God's goodness in her life, she cannot remain trapped in pity. Remembering God's blessings is the direct path to restored wholeness. We can say with the psalmist, "Hope in God; for I shall again praise him, my help and my God" (Psalm 42:11).

₴ *Extraordinary Living Is God's Plan*

Any plan that belongs to God has to be extraordinary. Take a look at some of the plans of God.

• Create the universe out of nothing.
• Keep the cosmos operating, turning and spinning and moving just right to provide day and night and summer and winter.
• Make stuff—like light, darkness, land, sea, stars, moon, sun, plants, fish, birds, and animals.
• Create human beings inside the wombs of other human beings.
• Design the world in technicolor instead of black and white.
• Turn a rod into a snake and water into blood.
• Divide a sea and provide dry ground so His people can walk through it.
• Cause food to fall out of the sky each day.
• Make a donkey talk.
• Stop the sun for three days.
• Send a big fish to swallow Jonah.
• Let three men walk around in a furnace when the fire is burning.
• Provide jars of oil that never run dry.
• Send Jesus to earth as a baby born of a virgin.
• Turn water into wine.
• Invite unwanted people to His banquet.
• Allow His Son to be crucified for those who don't deserve it.
• Adopt unworthy people into his family and share His inheritance with them.
• Become a contractor and build houses for people in heaven.

Nothing is ordinary when God gets involved. He thinks and acts in the spectacular. From the time I was a child I have been interested in the space program. As a junior in high school, I wrote an essay about the Saturn mission. My teacher submitted it to a national essay contest sponsored by NASA. I did not win anything, but the experience cemented in me a growing awe of mankind's ability to create a rocket that would travel to a distant planet, followed in a few years by men who put their feet on the moon. I am convinced that this was, and is, God's extraordinary work through ordinary people.

Extraordinary does not happen just on another planet or in the aerospace industry. Three years ago my daughter called me. "Mom, I want you to be in the delivery room when I have my baby." My response was "Are you sure? You know I don't do well when you are having pain!" "Oh, Mom, we'll help you," she responded cheerfully. (Yes, I am a real wimp when it comes to my daughter.)

A few months later, I flew to Denver for the birth of Nicolas. He was late, and late, and even later in arriving. Finally the doctor told me to take Michele to the mall and walk. So we did. We walked and walked and walked until we were both exhausted. We had covered every inch of the mall several times over. I enjoyed talking to her and laughing about her very pregnant condition as she grew more and more uncomfortable. Finally, the discomfort became significant and we hurried to the hospital.

Nicolas still took his time; but in the early hours of the morning, I held our third grandchild in my arms. He was adorable. I was there to experience his first cry, see him placed in his mother's arms, and see the joy in his father's eyes. The process of conception, expectancy, and delivery is extraordinary. From the time that humanity was in God's plan, He decided that every aspect of this life would be extraordinary. Who would not agree that blood pumping through our human system, delivered there by a heart that needs no electricity or gasoline, is extraordinary?

The preface in *Fearfully and Wonderfully Made* tells of the day Dr. Paul Brand showed his incomplete book manuscript to

Philip Yancey. Dr. Brand explained why he was writing a book using the human body as an analogy for Paul's New Testament teachings regarding the body of Christ. He said, "In a sense we doctors are like employees at the complaint desk of a large department store. We tend to get a biased view of the quality of the product when we hear about its aches and pains all day. In this little manuscript, which I set aside long ago, I tried to pause and wonder at what God made."

The world with all its troubles and sicknesses often hides from our minds the incredibility of our lives. The fact we exist at all is a marvel. Have you watched a birth? Have you seen how the body adapts to allow a small human being to enter the world? Have you seen the provision the body makes for that little human while it waits to be delivered?

God intends for life to be extraordinary. After all, nothing about God is ordinary, and He is the initiator and the sustainer of life. Whatever life exists has come from the hand of God alone. "I wish I had never been born" is a comment that most of us have heard, or maybe even said, during our lifetime. May our words to those in despair remind them that they exist because God wants them to exist and that their existence is an extraordinary reality, a true gift of God's love.

❧ Extraordinary Living Is Not the Way of the World

A man seated next to me on the plane told me that he had been watching me since I came aboard. He said something about me seemed different. As we visited, I had opportunity to tell him about my ministry. He responded by telling me that his life was empty. He had money, power, a wonderful wife, beautiful children, and everything that he had wanted in life. Yet he felt empty. "I don't believe in miracles," he said as he went on to tell about the blessings of his life and the joy of his family. "My wife and children are committed to God, but I don't believe in God." He described to me a woman of great inner and outer beauty and children of exceptional grace.

The door was open for me to tell the miracles I see every day, the miracle of someone who cares for another more than himself, or the miracle of forgiveness offered to one who has offended another. I told of seeing my grandchild come into the world. I mentioned the miracle of love that always expects the best and chooses to give rather than receive.

"Have you not seen any of these things in your life? As you described your family, I saw something unusual that transcends worldly ways and desires," I said. He was thoughtful. "I hadn't thought about that," he responded. "You are right. Something about them is exceptional."

I told him of Jesus Christ and the transformation He brings to our worldview. I told how Jesus reconciles us to Himself so that we are no longer the same people we were before. I explained that Christ in our lives is a miracle that restores us to the true humanity God intended for us to be. I mentioned that our disillusionment with life comes from our own disillusionment with ourselves. We think God is the culprit, but our own inner struggle against our Creator as He calls out our name is what causes our disillusionment. We fall for the lies of the world that would lead us to believe that whatever we cannot see does not exist and whatever we cannot control is not real.

An acquaintance has said that life treated him roughly. He mentioned his divorces and other situations that resulted primarily from his own choices. My friend said that these are the tribulations he has suffered for Christ. My friend has inappropriately equated the ways of the world with the suffering of Christ. Suffering for Christ can only happen when one is living for Christ. The joy, peace, and love that Christ offers are found in a life given to living as Christ lived.

How far is my friend from experiencing the extraordinary

life? Not far at all. Regardless of his confusion, God extends his forgiveness and extraordinary life to all who turn from the world and receive His wonderful gift. Read again the thrilling words of the apostle Paul from Ephesians 2:1-7.

"You were dead through the trespasses and sins in which you once lived, following the course of this world, following the ruler of the power of the air, the spirit that is now at work among those who are disobedient. All of us once lived among them in the passions of our flesh, following the desires of flesh and senses, and we were by nature children of wrath, like everyone else. But God, who is rich in mercy, out of the great love with which he loved us even when we were dead through our trespasses, made us alive together with Christ—by grace you have been saved—and raised us up with him and seated us with him in the heavenly places in Christ Jesus, so that in the ages to come he might show the immeasurable riches of his grace in kindness toward us in Christ Jesus."

❧ I Pray You Will Live the Extraordinary Life

I went with several women from my church to a training event for a women's organization called Woman's Missionary Union. I shared a hotel room with Sue, a friend who was a counselor by profession and a wonderful woman who had chosen to give her counseling expertise away to the community. She lived in another city some distance from mine. Her office was in a local church where she touched many lives in turmoil.

The second day we were there, I visited with Sue. I did not get to see her often and always enjoyed being around her. In the course of an ordinary conversation, Sue said, "Andrea, the Lord has led me to share something with you. Someday you are going to be the leader of our state organization. I know that this is true for the Lord has shown this to me." When I protested, she hushed me and stated with all resolution that her words would some day prove to be true.

Now there were many reasons this should not have happened. For one thing, we did not even have a state organization. Four years later our state formed its own organization. Also, while God had been good to me and my life seemed to be extraordinary already, I did not have the background I considered prerequisite for leadership, including education, status, and certain types of experience.

Four years later, I was in the meeting in which our state voted to form a new fellowship of churches. The thrill of seeing God at work as He called persons to step out and risk standing on their own is unforgettable. I still can hardly believe I witnessed this moment in my denominational history. Although I felt like an insignificant part of our new fellowship, I saw with my own eyes how the Lord grew our people and our churches. I saw the outstanding leaders God had equipped to guide us.

The process was set in motion. Just two years later the new state fellowship began operation. A few months before the beginning date, I received a call from the executive board of the new fellowship. The board offered me the very position in which Sue had told me five years earlier I would serve. Everything that Sue told me became a reality.

The Lord has not given me the exact details of your life in Him. I probably do not even know you. The one thing I can tell you about your future is that God gives ordinary people extraordinary lives. If you belong to God, then you are in the right place to experience the extraordinary life He offers.

My prayer for you is that this book will encourage you to accept God's offer of extraordinary life. My prayer for you is found in Ephesians 1:17-19.

"I pray that the God of our Lord Jesus Christ, the Father of glory, may give you a spirit of wisdom and revelation as you come to know him, so that, with the eyes of your heart enlightened, you may know what is the hope to which he has called you, what are the riches of his glorious inheritance among the saints, and what is the immeasurable greatness of his power for us who believe, according to the working of his great power."

The significance of this prayer is manifold. First, Paul asked that his readers receive "a spirit of wisdom and revelation" from God, the Father of glory. The wealth of who God is resides in this request. We have an all-wise, all-revealing Lord. He yearns for those who call Him Father to know more of Him and His providential guidance. Wisdom is that which guides us into the right way of life, the best way of life, the way that will make us whole and fulfilled.

God's wisdom is the only way our hearts can be enlightened. Wisdom draws the eyes of one's heart toward the cross. Wisdom opens our eyes to let light into the darkness. God penetrates the eyes of our hearts with knowledge of Him, drawing us so close that our lives cannot be separated from His—a relationship more intimate and real than that of the closest loved one.

When wisdom pushes away the darkness that blinds us to God's goodness, we discover hope, a unique hope, an intentional hope, "the hope to which he has called you." Paul said, "You have a reason to live." God has called you, and His call is not random or aimless. Rather, God's call for your life is that you will now have hope. You have been called from hopelessness to expectancy, expectancy for what God can do and will do in your life and through your life, culminating in His perfecting you so that you will become in the likeness of Christ.

John Stott, in *The Message of Ephesians,* wrote these words: "God called us to Christ and holiness, to freedom and peace, to suffering and glory. More simply, it was a call to an altogether new life in which we know, obey, and serve Christ, enjoy fellowship with him and with each other, look beyond our present suffering to the glory which will one day be revealed."

Yes, God has called us to Christ, and in Christ He has bestowed an inheritance on us. He wants us to know the "riches of his glorious inheritance" (Eph.1:18). Believe it or not, our inheritance is God Himself. The Father said that He will give you Himself. He will give you His personality. He will give you His character. He will give you His forgiveness, compassion, and grace, so that as you go through life you will not be alone. He will be with you. When you suffer trials or persecution, He will be there. When the ones you love break your heart, He will restore you. When you've made a mistake or taken the wrong turn, He will help you find the right way.

We have received an inheritance from God, and He has received an inheritance in us. Since before the foundations of the world, God's plan was that you and I could once again walk with Him in the garden. He is a giving God, a loving God, and He longs for fellowship with us. He yearns to give all that a loving Father has to give, for that is who He is toward us!

What kind of God is this who can bestow upon us so many riches and longs to be in a loving relationship with us? Our God is a God whose power is so magnificent and sufficient that He fears nothing. He is completely at ease in giving Himself away to us for He alone determines our days. When He takes the blinders from the eyes of our hearts, we discover that His power is sufficient for all our needs. God's power conquered evil when Jesus died on the cross. God's power conquered death when He raised Jesus from the dead and seated Him on a heavenly throne.

Now you understand more fully my prayer for you. Welcome to extraordinary living! Amen and amen.

Prepare for an Extraordinary Life

Preparation begins
On a heavenly plane,
Where a wonderful Father
Sees your birth as His gain.
He leaves nothing to chance,
Expects only good things,
So that in His own time,
You to Him will He bring.

Chapter Three
A Charismatic Personality

Perfection is Jesus,
God's model of human,
Christ's image of person,
For "Who am I?"
The answer.

everal years ago, everyone in my department took a personality inventory. After the inventory, we received the results for each person, with a description of the personality types, and a list of suggestions for how to communicate with each type. My immediate supervisor and I had a good relationship except for one situation that frustrated both of us: I presented many ideas expecting immediate enthusiasm. She, on the other hand, wanted time to process ideas before responding.

The scenario went like this: I would come into her office and verbalize my great idea, expecting a positive, excited response. She would look doubtful and send me back to the drawing board. I would leave feeling repressed, wondering at her lack of excitement. She felt badly that she had thrown a wet blanket on my creativity. We both knew this situation existed but neither of us knew just how to change it until we took the personality inventory.

I learned that she is a processor. She is practical, detailed, and deliberate. She likes to see detailed plans while I prefer to think on my feet, process in my head, and look at the big picture rather than the details. Once I discovered how she was different from me, I realized that if she were going to give my ideas any hearing I would need to present them in a way compatible with her personality. That is what I did. At the same time, she adopted some new approaches in responding to my ideas. The change was immediate. We both recognized how we could work with one another more effectively. Our already good relationship was strengthened.

ề Personality Is God's Gift

Personality does matter. Personality does not just happen. It has to come from somewhere, and the Source is God. God gives us each our own personality. Not only does God give us personality, but He makes them one of His best gifts to us. Someone once said, "God don't make no junk!"

Since personality is a gift from God, shouldn't we understand our personalities and feel good about who we are? Wouldn't it be good for us to understand one another's personalities so we could affirm one another and serve together effectively? If we learn to communicate better with our parents, siblings, spouses, children, and friends, won't we be more hopeful of seeing our lives move from the ordinary to the extraordinary?

When my husband Mike and I married more than 30 years ago, I did not realize that our personalities were on the opposite ends of the spectrum from one another. No wonder we have to work hard at communicating. We are *still* learning to communicate. He listens as I tell him every detail of my trips, and I accept his silence. He smiles at my enthusiasm, and I am amazed at how calm he is. He can be alone for days while I can only stand being alone for a few hours at a time. I affirm his routine, and he gives me surprises. The list of our differences goes on and on. Learning to communicate with him is worth the effort for we can look forward to many years of joy and love together and a marriage that is more than ordinary—maybe even extraordinary.

Understanding and appreciating our differences can result in real serendipities. I was out of town the week of our 32nd anniversary. When I got home, Mike told me to repack my suitcase because we were leaving for the night. Within minutes, he whisked me away to a downtown hotel where he had already prepared our suite with candles and gifts. He knows that I love surprises, especially when they are filled with romance and love.

Studying personality can be a complex issue because no one is exactly like another. When psychologists and scientists study the puzzling intangibility of the human person, the results are varied and in some ways ambiguous. Even so, experts agree that most of us fall into basic categories that overlap, but that provide a structure for improving relationships and communication.

The Business Resource Center uses Roger Birkman's "Colors" system from his book *True Colors* to assist persons in the corporate world in understanding and dealing with others. The Colors model is based on external behaviors that can be seen when relating to another person. Green, Red, Yellow, and Blue represent four different ways of communicating.

Recently my department asked our CEO to lead our group

through the "Colors" inventory. We discovered that we have a good mix of colors. I do not think any of us were surprised with the results, but we had fun as we compared our likenesses and differences along with our need for each other. I was surprised to discover that I had an equal amount of green, red, and blue, but not a smidgen of yellow. As you read on, you will discover what that means. Knowing that I have no yellow makes me especially thankful for the three women in my department who are yellows.

Most books on personality mention anywhere from four to nine types. For the sake of brevity I am using four, but I encourage you to read books that discuss personalities from various perspectives. As you look at personality types, do not be surprised if you find yourself saying, "but I find myself in all of these." Very few people are clearly one type, but I think you will see one or two personalities that are dominant in the person God has made you to be.

My goals for this chapter are that you will rejoice in the personality that God has given you, that you will appreciate other personalities, and that you will discover how God's character can make you a whole person. When you achieve these three goals, you will better understand how God takes ordinary women and gives them extraordinary lives.

❧ Four Personalities the World Needs

The Sympathetic
When Rose, who served in my department, left our organization, our team knew a big hole would exist. Rose was our strongest Sympathetic personality. Rose knew everyone's needs because she took time to listen and care. Whatever the situation, she made sure those who felt excluded were included. When our team gathered for a meeting, she brought encouraging note

cards and stickers for everyone. She served on the ministry team in our building and spent many of her off-work hours making sure ministry projects were completed as promised. She provided meals for the grieving and collected supplies for children in need. When any relationship was not as it should be, she fasted and prayed for all involved.

Rose had planned to become a nurse, but during nursing school she discovered she cried over every patient. She changed her vocation, but she still gave us advice. She would say in jest, "I am a nurse, you know." When others commented on her personality, those in our department would reiterate, "She is a nurse, you know!"

My sister Kathlyn has many Sympathetic attributes. Recently she told me that being at home with family was her greatest joy. As her big sister, I know that she is committed to her family and compassionate toward others.

A few months ago when our father was in an intensive care unit, Kathlyn, Mother, and I were leaving the waiting room as a man came toward us. He suddenly collapsed, incoherent and spitting up blood. Several people were in the hallway, and I ran to call a nurse. When I returned, a nurse had arrived with a cold cloth. My sister was sitting on the floor, holding the man in her arms as she held the wet cloth on his head. I thought she looked like an angel.

I am not surprised by her Sympathetic personality since I have seen the same in my mother who is a soft touch for any child or animal in need. For all of my growing up years, my mother modeled gentle concern toward others. By her example, she taught us how to care for animals. She taught us to send thank-you notes, to love our extended family, and to be kind in our speech. My mother has traveled with me several places in the world and managed to develop a fan club wherever we go.

Are you a Sympathetic? Check the statements that describe you and then total how many you checked.

_____ I am respectful of others.

_____ People often come to me with a need.

_____ I am supportive of others.

_____ I have a strong desire to please others.

_____ I prefer to avoid confrontation.

_____ I am agreeable.

_____ I am people-oriented.

_____ I enjoy sharing with others.

_____ Harmonious relationships are important to me.

_____ I am intuitive and can often sense who people really are.

_____ Total

One of four personality types that Florence Littauer describes is the phlegmatic, which is much like my Sympathetic. She writes that the phlegmatic personality has many friends because she is easy to get along with and is a good listener. The phlegmatic is a natural in relating to the other personality types. As a Sympathetic, you share this wonderful ability to make friends. You feel drawn to people, especially people in need. Whatever your vocation, at home or in the workforce, you most likely will find yourself in roles such as counselor, teacher, mediator, mentor, minister, or hostess.

The color blue used in the "Colors" system represents people whose communication style is considerate, friendly, and agreeable. Blues are people-oriented and non-assertive. You are likely to see these behaviors in the Sympathetic personality as well.

Former President Bush may be a Sympathetic personality. He has a people-focused approach to life. Bush is known for the notes he writes to his friends. Writing these notes has been an important factor in the large number of friends and avid supporters he has across our nation.

If you are a Sympathetic, nurture your natural ability to love people and make friends. Go with God into places where you will experience the extraordinary life He offers, as He works through you to meet the needs of others and bring comfort to hurting individuals.

The Meditative

Not too long ago, I was in several meetings with someone who appeared to be a Meditative. She usually arrived early and had everything in place for the meetings. She listened attentively and wrote all the while, even though she was not assigned to take notes. If anyone needed to know what we said or decided about a subject, she always knew. When she spoke she usually had good insight into the situation. She was conscientious about any task or assignment and could be counted on to follow through with her commitments.

Since I also work with several other Meditative personalities, I have noticed that they are perfectionists and often lead in solving logistical problems. They have strong organizational skills. They listen carefully, hear what is said, and record it. I am always amazed at how long they can stay at their desks before looking for a distraction. They are also careful to send cards and notes for every situation or occasion.

The "Colors" system identifies persons who are serious, methodical, and precise as Yellows. Yellows tend to be task-oriented and non-assertive in their communication style, which are common behaviors of Meditative personalities also.

Meditatives may be found in management, science, law enforcement, health care, education, and religious service. Their commitment to honesty and professionalism makes them desirable employees in positions that depend on trust.

Are you a Meditative? Check the statements that describe you and then total how many you checked.

_____ I can do it better myself.

_____ I learn from watching and reading.

_____ I am efficient and tend to be a perfectionist.

_____ I process ideas before accepting them.

_____ I sometimes appear inflexible.

_____ I enjoy being alone with my feelings and interests.

_____ I have a difficult time expressing my feelings.

_____ I enjoy routine.

_____ Details are important to me.

_____ I sometimes feel awkward around others.

_____ Total

If you are a Meditative, meditate on the quality of work God enables you to do and the insights He allows you to have. Reflect on the integrity with which you approach all of life. You are extraordinary.

The Logical

I often feel that I am surrounded by Logicals. Several people come to mind immediately, including my husband Mike. Logicals want to know: "How do you know it will work? Has it been tested? How much will it cost? Who is going to do it?"

Mike's guiding principle is found in the word *practical*. He has to see, feel, smell, taste, and hear before he believes something is a reality. When I tell him something is wrong with my car, he has to see the evidence for himself.

Mike is a Bible teacher in our church. His practical approach to life is seen in the way he systematically approaches the lesson, laying out the context of the biblical passage, an exposition of the Scripture, and a very practical application of the lesson to life. He can take a complex passage and make it come alive for everyday life. His practicality enables him to interpret God's Word for people who need from God a fresh message that is relevant to their lives beyond the church.

Are you a Logical? Check the statements that describe you and then total how many you checked.

_____ I am practical.

_____ I am analytical.

_____ I use facts to make a decision.

_____ Acting calm makes me feel stronger.

_____ I like to know the rules.

_____ I like order in my life.

_____ I like predictability.

_____ I have a dry sense of humor.

_____ I am an avid reader and enjoy becoming knowledgeable in specific subjects.

_____ I tend to be cynical.

_____ Total

In the book *Personality Plus*, Littauer's Melancholy personality is similar to my Logical. She mentions the thoughtful, analytical, chart-loving, detailed, orderly approach to life, along with a genius intellect. Logicals, or Melancholies, will find themselves filling roles such as problem-solvers, administrators, budgeters, designers, musicians, artists, or writers.

The "Colors" system uses Red to identify people who communicate in efficient, independent, and authoritative ways. I have noticed that when my department at work has a task, I can become quite Red in my behavior. I want everyone to stick to the task. Reds are task-oriented and assertive, which is also how a Logical is likely to communicate.

If you are a Logical, rejoice in the ability you have to bring order in a confused world and leave a lasting impact through your work at home or in the workplace. Go with God to use your often-astounding analytical ability to change the world. The Logical can have and enjoy an extraordinary life in God.

The Dynamic
I recently read a list that describes the way a Dynamic thinks. The list went like this:
• Give me companionship, affection, and freedom.
• Engage with me in stimulating conversation and laughter.
• Appreciate my grand visions and listen to my stories.
• Don't try to change my style. Accept me the way I am.
• Be responsible for yourself. I dislike clingy or needy people.
• Don't tell me what to do.
(From *The Enneagram Made Easy* by Renee Baron and Elizabeth Wagele.)

So goes the Dynamic personality. A friend of mine once told me she was looking for a man of this personality. She thought men with this personality were fun to be with and brought a sense of adventure to a relationship. Actually, many who are called into the pulpit ministry are Dynamics, persons who enjoy being in front of a crowd and are filled with stories to tell.

Dynamics usually think on their feet, move and act quickly, love excitement, are idealistic and futuristic, and persuasive. They can have a number of tasks going at any one time, are never bored if free to do their own thing, and are always ready for a new challenge. Actually, they prefer to initiate new things and allow others to pick up the details involved in keeping the old going.

When I look back on my growing up years, I realize that my

Dynamic personality was a tremendous asset since I moved often. I attended new schools and made new friends often. My feelings about that time are more positive than others whose families relocated when they were children. For me, every new place was a new adventure and a new challenge to be mastered. I seldom looked back, and I seldom kept the friends I left behind. I easily adapted to each place, and I remember very few places that I did not enjoy.

The "Colors" system uses green to represent persons whose communication style is outgoing, convincing, and enthusiastic. They are assertive and people-oriented. Green is definitely the color for the Dynamic personality.

Are you a Dynamic? Check the statements that describe you and then total how many you checked.

_____ I get excited easily.

_____ I am enthusiastic.

_____ I am busy and energetic.

_____ I like people, and I usually like myself.

_____ I tend toward the dramatic.

_____ I enjoy initiating new things.

_____ I prefer the big picture more than the details.

_____ I have many ideas and see many possibilities.

_____ I am idealistic and look for the best in people.

_____ Life is a party!

_____ Total

If you are a Dynamic, celebrate the joy you receive just from living each day. Keep your eyes open to the possibilities for changing the world around you for the better. Let your enthusiasm for life become an encouragement for others. You have every opportunity to participate in extraordinary living.

⮞ *God's Gift of Personality to You*

When you totaled items you checked, which of the lists had the highest number of checks? These brief introductions to personality are just a taste of what you could know about the person God has made you to be. Many books are available to increase your understanding of personality and to help you know how to more effectively relate to persons with different personalities. Actually, the more you enjoy personalities that are like yours *and* different from yours, the more potential you have for knowing the full personality of God.

The Perfect Personality of God

Philip Keller, in his book *A Gardener Looks at Fruit of the Spirit,* writes that God's people are like a carefully cultivated garden, which is tended and tilled with tender, loving care. The gardener is "God Himself in Christ by His Spirit." Our lives are exactly where God desires to abide. His plan for each of us is that our lives will become His home.

How amazing that God could live in so many differing personalities. How can He do that? Could it be that He is the ultimate personality and that all the wonderful traits He has given to us inhabit Him?

When Jesus took on human form, He showed us not only who God is but what being human means. He brought to life before our eyes the perfect personality of God, as it should be revealed through God's people. Jesus was all that is good about being Sympathetic, Meditative, Logical, and Dynamic. Yet He was even more. No wonder Jesus knew how to relate to each individual. Jesus understood the needs of Sympathetic John,

Dynamic Peter, Logical Martha, and Meditative Mary. Jesus knew what each of them needed to become completely whole in their personhood.

The apostle Paul knew that the human personality apart from God was less than whole. In his letter to the Christians at Galatia, he described exactly what God, the Gardener, is cultivating in our humanness to make us complete. Read Galatians 5:22–23.

"By contrast, the fruit of the Spirit is love, joy, peace, patience, kindness, generosity, faithfulness, gentleness, and self-control. There is no law against such things."

Paul described God's character. Wholeness is our personality combined with God's character. The extent to which our personalities reflect these fruits that come from God is equal to the measure of God in our lives.

The more we give ourselves over to God, the more our personality becomes like God's personality. The more of God's character our personalities take on, the easier accepting other personalities becomes. One can even embrace and enjoy them. Join me in seeing how God wants to bless the person you are with the person He is.

The Fruit of Love Is Yours
God's love drew Lulu Goodrick to Christ at age 65. Where did she see His love? She saw His love through the lives of the women she met in a weekly Bible study. Women who accepted her, expecting nothing in return, made her a part of their circle of friends and family.

God wants you to place your personality within the confines of His love. What is God's love? Philip Keller describes God's love with majestic beauty.

Among God the Father, God the Son Jesus Christ, and God the Holy Spirit, there flowed love in its most sublime form. In fact, this love was of such purity that it constituted the very basis of their beings. It was the essence of their characters.

We humans can barely conceive of a relationship so sublime that it contains no trace of self-assertion, no ulterior motive or self-gratification. That is the secret strength of God. Here was demonstrated the irresistible force of utter selflessness. In the total giving of each to the other, in profound caring for each other, lay the love of all eternity. This was love at its loftiest level. This was love at its highest source. This was love, the primal source of all energy.

—(From *A Gardener Looks at Fruit of the Spirit*)

God's love is completely void of fear, punishment, and guilt. Rather, God's love is strength for the day and hope that never gives up. Traveling across the beautiful state of Wyoming years ago, I was sharing with a friend that I received scholarships to college when I graduated from high school, but I squandered away the opportunity. As a result, I did not have a college degree. I wanted to serve God in new ways that called for the education I did not have. I saw little hope for a college education. I explained to my friend that I did not deserve another chance. My friend listened to my story before reminding me that God does not think like I do. He forgives, restores, and blesses. Even when we give up on ourselves, God does not lose hope. Contemplate the description of love from *The Living Bible* in 1 Corinthians 13:4-7.

"Love is very patient and kind, never jealous or envious, never boastful or proud, never haughty or selfish or rude. Love does not demand its own way. It is not irritable or touchy. It does not hold grudges and will hardly even notice when others do it wrong. It is never glad about injustice, but rejoices whenever truth wins out. If you love someone you will be loyal to him no matter what the cost. You will always believe in him, always expect the best of him, and always stand your ground in defending him."

I often return to the *Living Bible* interpretation to see love in the most practical terms. Read the passage again as you think that this is the way that God loves *you*. Not only that, this is the way that God enables you to love others when your personality is remolded by His love.

Love is yours. Love is poured into your life from the time you are born by a God who cannot keep from loving you. God is love and when He is present in your life, love spills over from you onto and into the lives of those around you. God loves you and loves others through you, an intangible experience with tangible results, all in God's plan for extraordinary living.

The Fruit of Joy Is Yours

Do you hear joy in the Acts 16 story of Paul and Silas praising God and singing in the prison jail? Reading the story moves me to want to be in their place, to experience the joy that overcomes all odds. Since I do not think they were happy about being thrown in prison, joy must be a unique reality that comes from confidence in God's ability to see us through any and all situations.

Joy is often gained and understood through suffering for Christ's cause. In fact, this heart and life identification with our Savior may be the pathway to a personality that glows from inside out with the true *chara* or biblical joy. Perhaps the greater the suffering for Christ, the greater is the growth of the fruit of joy in our lives.

If you have been rejected or wounded because of your love for Christ, or if you have shared Jesus with someone who was not interested, you have been where joy is born, nurtured, and experienced. When the world rejects your love for Christ, your only place of refuge is the loving arms of your Savior who is waiting to comfort you, bless you, and give you His peace. A biblical passage that confirms the marvel of joy through suffering is found in Acts 7:54-60, the stoning of Stephen. I hope you will read the entire chapter, but to get you started, here are verses 54-56.

"When they heard these things, they become enraged and ground their teeth at Stephen. But filled with the Holy Spirit, he gazed into heaven and saw the glory of God and Jesus standing at the right hand of God. 'Look,' he said, 'I see the heavens opened and the Son of Man standing at the right hand of God!' "

The face of Stephen must have reflected *chara,* and nothing less, as he beheld God and His Son Jesus. What an awesome moment, looking into the face of God. Stephen saw beyond all pain and humiliation that he was being handed right into the loving arms of God Himself.

Perhaps this is where believers can have the last laugh, so to say. At the moment that a believer seems by the world's standard to be struck down, defeated, humiliated, a supreme failure, and laughable because she trusted in God, she rises up with a crown on her head and the riches of God in her life.

A young mother stands in the middle of the living room. She sees toys scattered to the four winds, handprints on the walls, spots on the carpet, and stains on the sofa. At first glance, she thinks her life is in complete disarray. When her life is placed securely in the confidence that God is Lord of all she is and does, she will have joy that cannot be contained or restrained, joy that spills over through her eyes, her words, and her attitudes. When her little ones are nurtured in God's love and God's ways, joy is the only possible ending. What a great story is the story of joy.

Joy is yours. God laughs through you as you walk through the world knowing that He is sovereign over all things. As Philip Keller writes, "To know the true joy of the Lord, present always in profound, quiet, still, inner power, because of His presence within, is to have the capacity to triumphantly transcend all the turmoil of our times in strength" (from *A Gardener Looks at Fruit of the Spirit* by Philip Keller, Word Publishers, 1986). Joy is God's wonderful fruit for your life. There, within the confidence you have discovered through Jesus Christ lies your joy for every day in every situation.

The Fruit of Peace Is Yours

The pregnancy test did not come in a box that was purchased from a pharmacy shelf. Rather, the test came in the form of an angel. The pregnancy did not come nicely packaged within the confines of marriage. Rather it came from an encounter with the Holy Spirit. The pregnancy was not planned for and anticipated by family and friends. Rather it would be a shocking revelation that might destroy relationships and reputation. Even so, the young teenage girl Mary responded, "Here am I, the servant of the Lord; let it be with me according to your word" (Luke 1:38).

Mary received news that would bring great misunderstanding, rejection, and hurt, yet she completely gave herself over to God's love. She was the embodiment of Philip Keller's description of peace as the "selfless, self-giving, self-losing, self-forgetting, self-sacrificing love of God in repose despite all the adverse reverses of life."

Peace is the most sought after fruit; believers hunger to have it. Persons who do not seek God still long for peace. I heard the story of a great golfer who hit his ball into the rough. When he was clearing debris from around it, he accidentally knocked it. It rolled to a place where he could get a clearer shot. No one saw what happened, but he admitted it immediately. The mistake cost him a stroke, which cost him the game. When asked about the loss of the game and the money, he responded that he may have lost money, but he had no trouble sleeping at night. For him, peace was sought over all earthly treasures.

Peace keeps our hearts and minds safely guarded against the anxiety that characterizes the world. Such peace is far from passive. God's peace does not need to avoid life's issues for this peace comes with answers. God's peace is aggressively at work in bringing peace to a world in chaos. Jesus said, "Blessed are the peacemakers"—those who wage peace against aggression and hatred, making friends out of enemies, and lovers out of soldiers.

Only recently did I realize that Scripture gives us a reason for the need for peace in our lives and in our world. Chaos and anxiety are certainly enough of a reason, but an even greater reason is found in 1 Timothy 2:1–4.

"First of all, then, I urge that supplications, prayers, intercessions, and thanksgivings be made for everyone, for kings and all who are in high positions, so that we may lead a quiet and peaceable life in all godliness and dignity. This is right and acceptable in the sight of God our Savior, who desires that everyone to be saved and to come to the knowledge of the truth."

Peace is the setting in which we can hear God's call to salvation. Peace is the still after the storm when we see that God is faithful and we can trust Him with our lives. In the heat of the battle, whether it is from crime or war or anxiety, we turn to God in desperation. We seek His protection and deliverance, and He gives it.

When my husband and I were hiking in the mountains some years ago, we surprised a porcupine in the bottom of a gully. Up went the quills, and the standoff began. The porcupine planted his feet with no intention of giving way. We had to make a decision; risk his wrath and stay on the path that he was effectively blocking, or turn the cheek and go another way. Needless to say, we decided another path would be just as interesting as the one we were on.

Peace is the fruit Jesus identified when He taught us to turn the other cheek. Peace is the fruit that finds another way, that insists on a *win-win* ending rather than an *I win, you lose* conclusion. Peace is gracious in the face of anger.

Peace is yours. For all the reasons that Jesus came in human form, the Scriptures tell us He came for the cause of peace. At His birth the angels sang, "Glory to God in the highest heaven, and on earth peace among those whom he favors!" (Luke 2:14). In the final days of his life, He encouraged His followers with the assurance of peace. "Peace I leave with you; my peace I give to you. I do not give to you as the world gives. Do not let your hearts be troubled, and do not let them be afraid" (John 14:27).

The Fruit of Patience Is Yours

The very thought of the word *patience* upsets many of us. We just do not feel like we can go there. Not long ago, I downloaded a new driver from a Web site onto my computer and managed to completely destroy all the programming on my hard drive. I did not know what I had done, but I knew it was serious. When I turned off the computer and then turned it back on, nothing appeared on the screen. I have to admit that *peace* was not my most immediate reaction. *Panic* is a more descriptive word for how I felt. My greatest concern was that my husband kept all of our banking records on the computer, and I had no idea how recently he had backed up the information. I just hoped he would not walk in until I had the situation under control.

Fortunately for me, I have a computer technical assistance contract that gives me access to online human help twenty-four hours a day. I called and a young man named Michael answered. When I explained what had happened, he said, "Oh, no. You have major problems. You have wiped out your hard drive."

"What does that mean?" I asked.

"That means we have to completely remove everything from your hard drive, reprogram your hard drive, and reload all your software," he responded. I nearly had a heart attack. His answer was the beginning of a very long night, finally ending about 2:00 in the morning. Following his careful instruction, the computer was restored to perfect working order.

This young man went through hours of tedious, step-by-step, guidance with a person who had minimal technical computer experience. Rather than getting frustrated with my inability, he encouraged me, laughed with me, and made me feel that everything was going to be all right. Over and over he repeated, "I am not going to leave you until your computer is completely restored." Even when his time to go home at midnight passed, he never changed his attitude and never swayed from his commitment to my need.

I have not been as patient with my own husband. Although we are both amateurs, he has had less computer experience and training than I have. It takes me only a few minutes to get frustrated when Mike is hesitant to try something he has not done before. I assure you, I never said to him, "Dear, I am not going to leave you until you have learned how to do this." Actually, he can hardly wait for me to quit helping him since I am such an impatient assistant.

When looking into the root words for the Greek word for patience, *makrothumeo*, two words come together. One is a word for *temper* or *passion,* and the other is a word for *long distance.* When these words are combined, the resulting meaning is that of *temper or passion that can go a long way.* One commentary describes patience as was seen in Jesus: "His task was to bear with the weakness of men and to suffer without retaliation, imitating the kindness of God, which was intended to lead sinners to repentance."

Not long ago, a newspaper carried the story of a woman who had served in an inner-city ministry for years. She had minimal income and extreme odds that would defeat an ordinary person. The needs of the children around her were tremendous. Many thought the resources required to help them were limited. This woman saw the situation in a completely different light. She saw churches, individuals, and businesses where the riches of God were waiting to be tapped. She discovered energy, excitement, and fulfillment enough to get her through each day. She experienced heartache, disappointment, and frustration that added to her persistence to change children's lives and give them the beginnings that each child needed. When she died, she was ripe to overflowing with the marvelous spiritual fruit of patience.

Patience is yours. The wonderful fruit of patience is birthed in you and nurtured in you when you are in a situation beyond your control to change and yet requires your diligent presence and activity. Patience is grown in you as you seek the Lord's intervention and learn to trust His timing and His response. Patience is the persistent determination to see the need through, to do all that is within God's power and then to go on doing more for nothing is beyond God's power. Patience is ripe in you as you pull out all the stops just when Satan was sure He had defeated you, and you respond with a resounding "Jesus is Lord, and He is greater than he that is in the world!"

The Fruit of Kindness Is Yours

Seated at the desk in the intensive care waiting room was a woman from my church. Her name was Sara. She volunteered every week to bring comfort to those waiting to have a few minutes with beloved family and friends. When I saw her, I felt as though my family was not alone. Someone in that room cared about us.

Sara's presence was especially touching since I knew that she struggled with her own physical needs, having battled cancer for some time. She knew the pain, fear, and hope of everyone in the room because she had lived with it herself.

Sara kept families in touch with the doctors who would call. She was there as a presence for anyone who had a need of any kind. She cleaned the waiting area and offered a kind word or touch. On the days she came to serve and my family was there, she always spent time with us, encouraging and listening to us.

God's kindness surely covers Sara from head to foot. The first time I met Sara she was seeing to the needs of others. The wife of a man in our church had been killed in a car accident. I went to help with serving a meal for the family and met Sara. At that time, she was taking radiation therapy; but that did not keep her from lending a merciful hand.

Philip Keller is convinced that kindness is associated with mercy. "It is impossible to be kind without being merciful. It implies a deep and genuine concern for another."

My friend Barbara tells everyone that she does not have the gift of mercy; but every summer for more than 32 years, she has organized and taken a group of youth to minister to migrants who come to work in her state. She has touched the lives of hundreds through ministries she has done around the world. She is committed to youth, especially teenage girls, and their nurturing. She goes out of her way, gives up her personal time, raises money, and the list goes on of her sacrifices to do these ministries. If Barbara is not merciful, then she most certainly is kind.

Keller describes a person with kindness as one who "forgets his own personal preferences to proffer help and healing to another. At the price of inconvenience, labor, and personal privation he goes out quietly and without fanfare to bring pleasure to another. Sensitive to the sorrow and suffering of a struggling society, he undertakes to do what he can to alleviate this suffering. He tries to make the world a better and brighter place for those enmeshed in its pain and pathos."

In Matthew 11:30, Jesus described His yoke as kind for He took us out from under the bondage of sin and the law and freed us to live abundantly. Paul noted the kindness of God that reached out to us with forgiveness and made us members of God's family (Rom. 11:17–24).

Surely, kindness frees others from the bondage of this world. When my husband and I went to eat at a nice Italian restaurant, I left a leaflet designed to be left with a tip. The leaflet said "thank you" and included a few words about knowing Jesus as Savior. When the waitress came to our table, I handed her the leaflet along with our tip, told her how much we appreciated her good service, and started to leave. Before we had gone out the door, she came running to stop us. She told us that this was the kindest thing any patron had ever done for her. After hugging us both, she went back to work.

Kindness is a gracious response to life that we often do not adopt. Reuben Welch describes in poetic form our tendency to withhold kindness.

You know, we want to save ourselves
 and keep ourselves
  and hold ourselves back
as though the highest goal in life would be
    to look good in our caskets.
It's no special blessing to come to the end of life
    with love unshared,
      selves ungiven,
   activities unactivated,
  deeds undone, and emotions unextented.
(From *We Really Do Need Each Other: A Call to Community in the Church*, by Reuben Welch.)

Kindness emanates from our understanding of God's love for us and God's desire that we love one another. God's love is the motivation for kindness. In fact, 1 John 3:17 tells us that love of God cannot be separated from kindness.

"But whoever has the world's goods, and beholds his brother in need and closes his heart against him, how does the love of God abide in him?" (1 John 3:17 NASB)

Welch explains the intensity of the word *heart* in this verse.

It's really interesting that the translators must have been
  feeling very civilized
    at the time this was translated
because what it really means
  is "innards."
There is a real neat short word for it
  that I hate to use in public.
Have you heard of "splangkna level" dialogue?
Maybe New Testament people didn't know too much
  about physiology
    but they sure did know a lot about people
                  and where you feel it
                    when you feel it.
When you have had your feelings hurt,
                  where does it hurt?
And when you are heavy-hearted,
                  where does the weight rest?
Not in your heart,
  but in your "splangknas"—that's where.

Kindness is the response of God's people to the love that we experience in Christ. God's love is involved with us, moved by our need, compassionate toward our suffering to the very extent that He chose to give his life for ours. "We know love by this, that He laid down His life for us—and we ought to lay down our lives for one another" (1 John 3:16).

Kindness is yours. You will find it in the reality of God's love for you, packaged in the good gifts He is pouring into your life that you in turn can pour into another's life. Encouraging words for a discouraged mind, good food for a hungry body, faithful friendship for a lonely heart, or the message of eternal salvation for a lost soul are just some of the ways that those who received God's kindness can extend His kindness beyond themselves.

The Fruit of Goodness Is Yours

A science fiction movie tells of a good scientist who creates a potion that enhances the *essence* of the person who takes it. The scientist is forced by the evil antagonist to drink the potion. When the good scientist takes it, he becomes stronger and truer. The adversary in the story is a man who wants to control the world. When he sees what happens to the scientist, his over-inflated ego assumes that his genius and good looks will be greatly enhanced. What he does not understand is that the potion responds to the being's true inner essence. Rather than becoming handsome and super smart, the antagonist becomes horribly disfigured, cruel, and vicious.

When I watched this movie I could not help but wonder what I would look like if I drank such a potion. What is my true essence? Who am I at the very core of my being? The fruit of *goodness* speaks to the substance of our nature. Read again what Jesus said about being good.

"As he was setting out on a journey, a man ran up and knelt before him, and asked him, 'Good Teacher, what must I do to inherit eternal life?' Jesus said to him, 'Why do you call me good? No one is good but God alone'." (Mark 10:17–18).

Jesus knew that all that is good, all goodness in itself, comes from God. God is good, all good. In Him, we can find nothing other than good. His essence is purest goodness. If we are to be good, we can only do it by allowing God into our inner most being. From God alone comes goodness.

Goodness is different from good deeds. Many people with little interest in God receive recognition for good deeds, including persons who risk their lives to save another or those who give millions of dollars to finance various services for persons in need. Anyone can do a good deed, a deed that helps another person. Good deeds come from any number of motives, and I believe that God uses both those who love Him and those who do not love Him to accomplish His good purposes in the world. Even so, good deeds alone are not evidence that a person is indeed good.

So what is goodness? Keller describes goodness as "lofty ideals, noble purposes, strong character, reliable conduct, and trustworthy integrity." I would go on to say that the lofty ideals are heavenly in nature, always concerned with drawing persons toward God.

A good person is one whose motive, mindset, and task in life is to provide only those words, acts, and thoughts that will turn others to God's purposes for their lives. A good person can be held up to the brightest light of scrutiny and the sun will come shining through. They have nothing to hide. When they speak good and kind words, the words are reflective of their hearts and minds toward others. How they act is the same whether others can see them or not.

In chapter one I mentioned a young, handsome man in our community who was arrested for murder. Strangely, this man was generally friendly, considerate, and glad to see you come into his shop. One day I was with an elderly friend going into a restaurant to have coffee when this man came by us. I don't remember the exact words he spoke, but what I do remember is tremendous cruelty in his eyes and mannerisms, a side of his character that I had never seen before. His words were cutting and demeaning toward my friend, a woman of great integrity and one to whom younger adults were highly respectful. My friend had known him since childhood, and she responded with all gentleness. His behavior demeaned him while my friend became ever more gracious in my eyes. After that day, I was uncomfortable when I encountered his false kindness, never dreaming that he would soon be convicted of murdering an entire family and eventually end up on death row.

How many times have we seen individuals enter the political arena only to be destroyed as their lives are scrutinized and the truth of their character is revealed? Is not this the stuff of which movies are made, as we are kept in suspense to see if a person is really who he says he is, or if we will discover that he has a completely different side to his character? Is not the desire of our Christian lives to allow God to enter us to such an extent that our lives reflect only God's goodness which becomes the motive for all our decisions and behaviors?

Goodness is yours. Your Father in heaven longs to give you His goodness. He knows that lives motivated by goodness will result in the greatest sense of esteem as we no longer seek to hide those parts of our thoughts and values that embarrass us. Esteem comes as we feel freer to reveal our truest selves to the world around us. Only as we feel good about our most hidden motives will we be ready to be "real" before the world.

The Fruit of Faithfulness Is Yours

A military officer grieved over the suffering of his household servant. The servant was paralyzed and in tremendous distress. The officer had already exhausted the abilities of the medical facilities in his area and now had only one place to turn. He went to Jesus for he was convinced that Jesus had the power to heal his servant.

Jesus listened to the officer's plea and the officer's declaration of faith. Jesus' response was one of amazement. Can you imagine a faith that would amaze Jesus? How deep, how strong, how vivid must the officer's faith have been? Jesus said, "Truly I tell you, in no one in Israel have I found such faith" (Matt. 8:10).

Faith is the entry point into the promise of God. Faith is the point at which we put our lives into the hands of another Who should be God. God's faithfulness to us is the same faithfulness that enables us to put our faith in Him.

What does God's faithfulness look like? According to the psalmist, the Lord's faithfulness extends to the heavens (Psalm 36:5). In other words, God's faithfulness encompasses the breath of the universe and the span of time. His Word is sure from before the foundations of the earth were put in place and will still be the same throughout eternity. Time has proven that God keeps His Word and that what He says will be fulfilled for us and in us. Faithfulness is an unchanging commitment, a sameness of mind toward another that never waivers.

God's faithfulness means that He remains true to His character. We can bank on His love, justice, compassion, and grace. He will not surprise us with a temper tantrum. He will not suddenly approach us with hatred, injustice, coldness, and a demand that we repay Him for His goodness. What assurance the Christian believer has in our God.

The interesting result of our trust in God is that it changes our attitudes toward the people around us. When we believe that God is who He says He is and that He will accomplish what He promises, then we also believe that He is changing lives and can achieve His plan in the lives of those we know. We begin to expect the best of others and believe in them. We care more deeply for their needs as we anticipate what God is already doing. Keller writes that we see people the way God sees them. "His love is being shed abroad in our hearts, so now we discover and discern the potential locked up in people. Our faith is not in their peculiarities but in their possibilities. With faith we believe and know and are assured that under God they can become great and noble."

Faithfulness is yours. You turn all that you are and have over to the God who has proven to be faithful to you. You commit your plans to Him and walk only where He leads. You wait for His guidance and His affirmation. You trust His plan for the world and boldly proclaim it and work with Him in it for you know that He will see it through and that He will see it through in a way that is the best for all who love Him. You do not worry if your children follow Him to distant lands for you know that they are in the hands of the One who is pure love and grace. You know that you will be kept in the palm of His hand, protected and carried on eagle's wings, and for you the deserts will blossom and the dry streams will flow with abundant water. Best of all, you know that you and many others will reach completion, and on that day you will be like Jesus. You will see Jesus as He is, and in the end, your God will reign over all the earth.

"Great and amazing are your deeds, Lord God the Almighty! Just and true are your ways, King of the nations!" (Rev. 15:3)

The Fruit of Gentleness Is Yours
Gentleness is like fabric softener, for all who come within the bounds of its touch feel soothed and comforted. The wrinkles of life seem to disappear in its wake. I have seen this happen when my grandchildren turn to their mother in times of distress. Her gentle caress and soft words calm their anger, hurt, and frustration.

Gentleness comes from a humble heart. In a contemporary movie, a little dog is thrust into the apartment of a man who does not like him. The little dog flattens himself on the floor and crawls toward the man, the picture of humility. Gentleness is willing to stoop as low as necessary to bow before the needs of another. I think the Asian custom of bowing has this thought in mind, with each person seeking to bow lower than the other to reflect his or her submission. Gentleness frees us to step down from our positions of authority and power, to take the hands of those around us and give them a helping hand, regardless of the situation. Every Scripture that speaks of gentleness includes the idea of humility. The reality is, apart from humility, gentleness cannot be experienced. If you have seen a truly gentle person, you probably agree that this person is also humble.

Gentleness includes the attitude of grace or extending care beyond what is deserved. The higher the stakes, the harder remaining gentle can be. Those of us who serve in stressful careers often find it difficult to stay gentle when we are at tables debating the direction our companies should take or getting our proposals pushed through. When we are rushing through life and we perceive that the persons around us are slowing us down or keeping us from achieving our goals, we often choose to force the situations and force the individuals to action. How wonderful when we can stop to see the need of those around us and find a way to bring them along without anger or intimidation. Even when we need to take a firm stand, we can handle the situation with gentleness and often reclaim or reenergize those around us. The discouraged find encouragement. The devalued once again feel worthy.

Gentleness often means slowing down and taking time to really see the people around us. We often assume situations to be one way when they may not be. We overreact only to discover that most of what we thought was not the actual truth. Since I tend to move and act quickly, I have to work at slowing down, taking time to listen and learn, thinking through the consequences, and deciding how to best achieve the results I want. Slowing down gives us time to hear, to consider the effects of our actions and words, to do what is best for all involved, and to allow the best outcome in every situation.

Gentleness is strength rather than weakness. Weakness has to tear down, but strength builds up. Weakness destroys those around a person while strength enables. Interestingly, when we overreact or lose our cool, we give up our power and lower our esteem in the face of others. The gentle person gains power and is admired and sought after by all who know her.

Gentle-living is an everyday decision that must be practiced over and over again as we feel God's gentle Spirit urging us to be more like Him. Didn't Jesus say, "I am gentle and humble in heart" (Matt. 11:29)? When Jesus stood beside the woman accused of adultery, turned in the crowd to reach out to the woman with a long-term physical illness, or stopped the moving parade to touch a blind man's eyes, we see how the work of gentleness looks in our world.

Keller says of gentleness that "out of an enormous, overflowing, spontaneous sense of thanks and gratitude we should be able to go out and live before others in humility and gentleness, serving them in sincerity and genuine simplicity. As the Father sent the Son into the world, so He in turn sends us out to serve in a sick society."

Gentleness is yours. As you extend your hand to reach out and lift up the heartbroken and the sin-sick, as you choose the healing word over the tearing word, as you help carry the burden that was not of your making, you are offering the gentleness of Christ to a hurting world. God offers to fill you with gentleness that will overflow in healing mercies to those around you.

The Fruit of Self-Control Is Yours

One day our neighbor showed up on our doorstep with her dog under one arm and everything we needed to take care of the dog under the other. The dog's name was Ruffles, and she was out-of-control. She had come from a bad environment to our neighbor's home. Our neighbor could not take Ruffles's bad behavior any longer, and she knew that I thought the dog was cute. When I opened the door, she said, "Take her. She is yours! I've had enough!" On that day Ruffles the out-of-control dog became a member of our family.

When I say out-of-control, I mean that this dog would not respond to any type of affection, guidance, or instruction. She would not even respond to her name when called. If we opened the door for any reason, she bolted out of the house and ran as fast as she could to nowhere. We spent many hours roaming the streets of the city looking for that dog.

One day Ruffles disappeared for a few hours. When we finally found her, she was one very sick puppy. A visit to the veterinarian revealed what the vet described as "garbage-gut," a tummy full of who-knows-what that she had found in a trash can. We did not think she would ever recover from that.

We pampered, loved, and cared for Ruffles. Yet she would run from us and run wild despite our love for her. We could not understand what was happening in her mind to cause such behavior. For two years, Ruffles ran away at every opportunity and was a generally unpleasant dog. Although she was cute at times, her personality was not so great. (After a visit to the groomer, we were informed that our dog was obnoxious.) Our love almost caved in several times, but for some reason we hung in with her.

Finally, without explanation, Ruffles quit running away. Not only that, we could not get her to go anywhere without us. She began to follow our commands and to respond when we called her name. Her personality was always strange, but we grew to love her ever more deeply as she responded to our care. Ruffles was like a member of our family, and for seventeen years we enjoyed her company.

The Lord wants to enjoy our company. He brought us into His family so He could love us, care for us, and give us guidance that would fill our lives with joy. Of course, to be effective, we must respond to His love, care, and wisdom. "I am yours, Lord, heart, soul, mind, and body."

Self-control is yours. As a Christ-follower, self-control is realized in God's control of your life. God will enable you to keep from running wild or filling your life with trash. God does this for His children. He will bring order out of your chaos and change your desires. You, just like Ruffles, will find a home that you do not want to leave and a place where your every need is met.

❧ Becoming a Whole Person

Your personality is God's wonderful gift to you. God's character is also His wonderful gift to you. Think about the personality type that is *you*. What does a Meditative look like when she also is abundant in the fruits listed in Galatians 5:22-23? What about a Sympathetic? A Logical? A Dynamic? How will you be able to tell that your personality is now completed with God's character?

If you are a Meditative, reflect on the possible results. If you are a Sympathetic, discuss this with a friend. If you are a Logical, make a list of the changes you will be able to see. If you are a Dynamic, write a speech about it. What might God have planned for your life? What will He accomplish through you now? Your wholeness is God's gift for extraordinary living!

Chapter Four

Talents and Skills in Abundance

Somewhere in the marketplace
A living's being made;
A woman does what's needed,
Regardless of the trade.
Because she cares, she does her best,
Knowing all the while,
Whatever skill the need requires,
She'll go the extra mile.

My daughter Michele is one of those rare adults who gets down on the floor with children, plays with them for hours, plans special activities to nurture their minds and bodies, and makes them the priority of her life. Her home is a place where any child feels welcome and loved.

I will never forget visiting her at her summer job in a church day-care center during high school. She was surrounded by nearly 20 two-year-olds. In the short time I was there, nearly every child in the room demanded her attention in some way. One visit was enough for me, but she had nearly endless energy and compassion for every child in the room. Now she has children of her own, and I know that when her own children reach adulthood, they will call her "blessed." Watching her has taught me much about motherhood.

Michele's natural talent for working with children is just one area in which she has obvious ability. She is a relaxed and fun hostess and lives with an open door to anyone who needs a friend. She can write a letter or a card that sounds as though it came from a Hallmark store. She has many friends in many places, and she stays in touch with them all.

Michele is also bold, not hesitant to speak against injustices and evils in the world. I have never seen her back down when an issue affected the rights, life, or well being of others. No doubt, she will be able to stand in the gap as an advocate for those who cannot help themselves.

My sister Kathlyn is also a woman of many talents and skills. From an early age, her natural artistic ability was evident. Not only is she creative, she is also naturally organized and detailed. Her talents opened doors for her to develop skills such as homemaker, hostess, banker, artist, and travel consultant. Her painted sweatshirts are works of art; her home is decorated and organized to perfection; and she excels in the workplace.

Then there is my mother. We moved often when I was growing up, and my mother turned every new place into a home and a school. She was decorator, educator, seamstress, hair stylist, physician, financial planner, chef, and counselor. Although she was mother and homemaker for many years, she later owned and operated a mini-mall with my father. She was chief operating officer and business manager while at the same time using her skill with children to teach preschoolers in church. Preschoolers often sat next to her in worship service with their parents' blessing, mainly because they behaved better for my mother. How her church appreciated her on Sunday mornings!

One of the gifts my mother gave to us was herself. She was available to us. Not only was she available, I now realize that she put our needs before her own. She showed her love for us by providing everything she could give to enable us to grow to our greatest potential.

As women, the creativity of God in designing us is unlimited. Few, if any of us, recognize how many natural abilities we have been given and how may skills we have learned, either from necessity or interest. A quick walk through our homes or workplaces reminds us of many skills and talents that seldom come to mind. A display of photos on a table, a bed made to look inviting, a green plant flourishing in the living room, a clean bathroom, a scrapbook of memories, or an organized closet or filing system, are visible symbols of natural talents and learned skills.

Someone said that with the talents and skills required to run a home, a woman could run the world. Like my mother, most women become teachers, bankers, administrators, nurses, negotiators, tailors, barbers, interior designers, carpenters, bus drivers, repairmen, security guards, chefs, trash collectors, and housekeepers in the process of building a home. All these skills and others seem built into the role of woman. The skills needed to live the life of an ordinary woman have always been multitudinous.

We know all things come from God. It makes sense that talents and skills are also of His doing. Some years ago, I had the opportunity to work with a group of Christians who encouraged God's people to see how God uses talents and skills in His plan. Through my involvement with this group, I discovered a reality about the Bible that I had not noticed before. It enhanced my perception concerning the relevance and value of Scripture to everyday life.

What I discovered is that most of us look at the stories of people in the Bible as stories of people who were more spiritual than we are, or larger than life. We do not view them for who they really were, ordinary working people. Bible stories center around the workplace and the home, ordinary people going about their daily business, through whom God often did extraordinary things. The Bible tells of people with talents and skills, how they used their talents and skills, and what God did with talents and skills of ordinary people when combined with His power and call.

Let's look at a few ordinary people from the Bible to whom God gave extraordinary lives. I think you will see in their stories several truths that are applicable to your life, whether in your home or in the workplace.

ॐ *From Ordinary to Extraordinary in the Home*

Eunice was one of the *ordinary* women of the Bible. She was a Hebrew woman who lived in the first century after Christ. Her husband was Greek, and indications are that he was not a Christ-follower. Eunice was married to a man of another culture and another religious faith.

Eunice's home was likely a blend of Greek and Hebrew traditions. Greek homes were orderly and education was valued. Eunice may have had responsibilities for entertaining and for managing servants. She may have had duties of handling the household accounts and keeping the home in working order. She may have had little formal education but must have been a role model for her son Timothy. Scriptures make it clear that Eunice created an environment that enabled Timothy to flourish. She may have been organized and hospitable, a good cook, able to prepare meals from both Greek and Hebrew recipes. She may have made the linens and clothing for the family and special gifts for important occasions. Perhaps she was a gardener and kept fresh cut flowers on her table. The apostle Paul must have been impressed with the upbringing Timothy received from Eunice for he reminded Timothy of the example he experienced through her life. Eunice used what God had given her to bring honor to Him in her home. God gave an ordinary woman an extraordinary life.

🙚 *Other Biblical Passages of Women in the Home*

The Bible underscores the value of women in the home. Titus 2:4 instructs women to take care of their families and their homes. Surely this call to women is based on the assumption that women have talents and skills that can be used to take care of families and homes.

A popular passage in Proverbs 31 mentions several talents and skills that are common and desirable in women. I've listed a few from the passage. Do you see yourself in here? What would you add to this list when you're reading the passage?

Talents and Skills in Proverbs 31
- Has knowledge of fabrics
- Able to work with her hands
- Discerning about food she serves
- Insightful in her purchases
- Early riser
- Cooks for her family
- Plans the work that needs to be done at home
- Wise investor in property
- A gardener
- Takes time for physical exercise
- Sales woman
- Hostess to those in need
- Weaver of fabric

- Seamstress for her family
- Teacher of wisdom and practical knowledge
- Hard worker
- Pray-er

An interesting Scripture search is a study of the stories of women and the skills they used to help their families. Women are often shown in a positive light as taking action in whatever way is needed to solve a problem related to their homes. A widow in Zaraphath gathered sticks to cook a final meal for her son and herself. Confronted with the need of another, she chose to please God. As a result, she had all the food that she and her family needed (1 Kings 17:8–24). The wife of one of Elisha's co-workers bravely found a way to keep the creditors from taking her children. Her actions allowed God to perform a miracle of provision in her life (2 Kings 4:1–7). A Shunammite woman was a woman of decision in a crisis. Her trust in God led to the restoring of her property at a later time (2 Kings 4:8–37; 8:1–6). In Proverbs 31, King Lemuel quoted a wisdom oracle taught to him by his mother. The oracle instructed him to avoid moral failure. His mother's oracle reveals the kind of woman that the remainder of Proverbs 31 describes.

In the New Testament, Jesus' mother gave guidance to her Son throughout His life and then was present in His moment of greatest need (Luke 2:19,48–52; John 2:1–12, 19:25–27). Women who were Jesus' friends prepared the ointments and spices for his burial (Luke 23:55–56). In Acts 9, Dorcas is praised for using her home to make clothing for widows. Her death led to such an outpouring of grief and concern that Peter made a special trip to pray her back to life (Acts 9:36–43).

These are stories of women who through their roles as homemakers, family members, and friends discovered that God uses ordinary women in extraordinary ways right where they live.

From Ordinary to Extraordinary in the Workplace

A shoeshine shop at Logan Airport in Boston was owned and operated for many years by an uneducated man who loved the Lord. As he polished shoes from around the world, he shared his hope in God. His tables held Christian tracts, and he prayed for those in need. His service and testimony touched many lives, and he led a number of people to commit their lives to Christ.

A few years ago the man died. His work and ministry in the Logan Airport was so valuable that his wife, highly educated and in a successful career, resigned to take over the shoe-shine shop so the witness for Christ could continue. She willingly changed from corporate executive to shoe-shiner. She knew that God takes ordinary skills and uses them in extraordinary ways. Who would have dreamed that a man who polished shoes could touch so many of the world's elite with an eternal significance? How many in the world would understand his wife's choice?

What an encouragement for those of us who feel we do not have special talents or skills. You see, it was God's decision to provide a place for the shoe shine shop in one of the most visible areas of the airport. It was God's plan to use the skill of shoe shining to bring the message of His love to a lost world. The skills are not the point. The point is that God is willing to do the extraordinary with whatever skills we have. If we can remember that, we will have confidence that whatever our skills, God will use them in extraordinary ways.

The Story of Lydia

The CEO called Lydia into his office. She was somewhat concerned since this was not his usual practice, especially with the women in the company. She knocked on the door and entered the lavishly decorated executive suite.

"Lydia, you are our top sales executive here in Thyatira. We would like to send you to Philippi to expand our business there." Lydia was thrilled with the opportunity.

Arriving in Philippi, Lydia discovered quickly that this was not a God-fearing community. She began meeting by the river with a group of women who loved God. They met every Sabbath to pray and to worship God.

As for her business, Lydia found a huge market for her purple dye, one of the most expensive dyes of her time and a mark of wealth or royalty. Purple cloth was in demand to adorn emperors and decorate temples. Ranked in value with gold, it was used for both tribute and international trade.

Lydia no doubt greatly influenced the lives of those to whom she sold purple dye, as well as to her co-workers and family. She must have been wise and skilled in closing sales. She probably had presence and had learned how to enhance this in the way she dressed and spoke.

We know that Lydia is the first recorded believer in the West, and that the first church in Europe met in her home. She met Christ by the river and immediately opened her home to her new Christian friends. As a result of her hospitality, all of her household became believers and her name has gone down in history as a church starter. Today, groups of women begin Bible studies in their homes with the intention of establishing churches, and many of these groups use Lydia's name to distinguish their ministry. Lydia used what God gave her in talents and abilities to honor Him in the workplace. God gave an ordinary woman an extraordinary life.

The Bible tells of women who worked as prophetesses and judges (Judges 4:4), midwives (Ex.1:18–21), reapers (Ruth 2:21–23), servants (Matt. 26:69–71), seamstresses (Prov. 31:24), and professional mourners (Matt. 9:23). Other work, such as basketweaving and candymaking, was also common for women, although not mentioned specifically as being done by women. Women with Jesus helped provide financial support (Luke 8:1–3) which most likely came from their own vocations. The treasured passage for model womanhood, Proverbs 31, states that the capable woman "perceives that her merchandise is profitable" and "makes linen garments and sells them; she supplies the merchant with sashes."

Women are richly talented and are able to develop endless skills to enrich lives. God places women in the workplace just as He places them in the home. Wherever He leads, His intention is that they experience the extraordinary life.

Now that we have explored biblical models of women in the home and in the workplace, we have a foundation on which to explore how we discover and develop our talents and skills, whether we are at home with family, working of necessity, or pursuing a career.

⋙ *Discovering Your Skills and Talents at Home*

I think Laura was born with the interior-decorating gene. She decided to make her condominium look like a tearoom, and it does. The colors are bright yellow and deep red. Birdhouses, "Sound of Music" memorabilia, floral prints, and wallpaper borders all add to the ambiance of her home. I thought that if I were Laura, I would charge people to eat with me!

My friend Linda now balances the checkbook in her home. After years of never knowing just how much money was in the bank, she and her husband both admitted that accounting was just not his skill. Since Linda began handling the bookkeeping, the whole family's stress is reduced. Now they know how much money they have even if it has not increased their income.

Delores has a backyard garden. Her crops do so well that she shares the abundance with her friends. Her meals often include fresh vegetables and unique varieties that are not commonly found at the store. She inspired me to try growing a few things on my deck, which resulted in a nice crop of bright red tomatoes.

Michele developed a chart to help her children learn to do their daily chores. The chart is posted on the side of the refrigerator, and each child gets to mark off the chores completed. A defined goal and reward is achieved when a chore has been done faithfully for a specific amount of time. Her children learned a variety of housekeeping skills and had fun in the process. When reward time arrived, everyone celebrated the joy of a job well done.

Each home is unique. Depending on our lifestyles, our time at home varies. For some, home is where they would rather be more than anywhere else, while others prefer to see the world. The people who live with us—children, parents, roommates— also define home. When living alone, the ways we use our skills and talents may differ from when we have other people in the house who are dependent on our care and attention.

Regardless of your situation, you have numerous skills and talents that add value to your experience of home. Many are probably taken for granted, such as the ones I have listed below. Notice the skill or talent used in parentheses. While you are already using most of these, you may have others you have not considered.

Life Responsibilities
1. Balances the check book (bookkeeping)
2. Uses the right color schemes and furniture (interior decorating)
3. Keeps the closets orderly (organizing)
4. Makes visitors feel welcome (hostessing)
5. Creates food that is appealing to eat and tastes good (cooking skills)
6. Keeps everything clean (housekeeping)
7. Keeps everything in working order (repairing things)

The home is a terrific place to try new things and discover what you can do. God's design for the home is that it will be a safe place to grow. Often we think this is just for the children in the home, but it is actually a place for all ages to expand their possibilities. When my daughter and her family moved into their first home, she discovered that their 30-year-old house needed lots of loving care. She has learned to do many things that would have involved great cost if done by a professional.

Recently she decided to paint the room where her guests stay. She bought the supplies she needed and ended up with a beautiful room she had done with her own hands. She learned a new skill and added to the value of her home. Best of all, she blessed her family as well as guests who stay there.

For Christmas a couple of years ago, I wanted to do something special for the women in my family. I do not consider myself a crafty person, but I decided to try an idea I saw in a magazine. I bought antique silver-plated spoons, dark and white chocolate, gold cord, and clear cellophane. After dipping the spoons in the dark chocolate, I drizzled them with the white chocolate. They were beautiful. I then wrapped each one in the clear cellophane and tied it with the gold cord. Under the tree at my sister's home were six special spoons with gold tags expressing my love and appreciation for each recipient.

My husband and I have a group of church friends who visit us often. They love my apple pie and pecan pie. When they come over to our house, what do you think we serve? Of course! Apple pie and pecan pie. I have cultivated this skill through the years, and I love sharing it with friends!

Using your skills and talents at home can change a life, change society, bring a smile, express love and concern, meet a need, or just be doing something you enjoy. God is a God of creativity and the giver of talents and skills. You have many, and home is a wonderful place to discover them.

❧ Discovering Your Skills and Talents in the Workplace

At 5:00 A.M. each workday morning, my alarm goes off. I am up and going, a little faster on some days than on others. My first paid job in life was baby-sitting when I was a teenager. From there I progressed to managing a trucking office, waitressing in a pizza parlor, driving as an escort for a pipe company, and assisting in managing a hardware store and a barbecue restaurant. Next I managed a program for a statewide ministry. Then I served as a consultant for Woman's Missionary Union (WMU), the largest Protestant women's organization in the world.

Now I am directing the consulting department for the same organization. With each position, I brought along my natural talents and abilities as well as skills I had learned. I am just beginning to learn how to hire new staff, develop staff, and prioritize staff work for the most strategic value to the organization.

What you do not see in the above list are the volunteer positions I held in my church and community. As a result of these non-paying jobs, I had numerous opportunities for training and for trying and developing new skills. They were invaluable! Through these roles I've learned to teach, to plan, to administer a program, to work with volunteers, to serve on planning teams. I've learned to lead a conference, to develop training and teaching plans, to speak in front of large and small groups, to travel on my own, to plan trips and events, to find needed resources, to counsel, to make posters, to work with people who have special physical and mental needs, to do yard work, to help build a house, to teach a person to read and write English, and the list goes on.

When my sister decided to move into a new vocational field, she enrolled in training to learn a travel industry computer program. The training was intense, but she now has a position with many benefits for which she was looking. During the time that she has been with the company she has participated in more training to develop her knowledge and skill in areas that have already opened doors for her to advance.

Using talent and skill in the workplace is not the end in itself. When women who love God go into the workplace, they go under the mantle of Hebrews 2:7, which quotes Psalm 8:4-6. "You have made them for a little while lower than the angels; you have crowned them with glory and honor, subjecting all things under their feet."

This passage from the book of Hebrews is the affirmation that God has given us authority over the world. In the workplace we bear the image of God. God has made us to work, just as He worked in creation and is working now. We are working beside God, going with Him to bring hope and justice and goodness to a hurting society.

The Word in Life Study Bible explains it in this way: "Your job can help accomplish that mandate, as you use you God-given skills and opportunities. He views your work as having not only dignity, but purpose and direction as well. He wants you to accomplish meaningful tasks as you labor with a Christlike work ethic."

When you are asked to learn a new skill at work or encouraged to develop a skill that you already have, both you and your employer are rewarded. Whatever your area of responsibility, training will broaden your base of knowledge and ability. My employer at the pizza parlor soon trusted the closing up of the restaurant into my hands. I learned to be responsible for seeing that the equipment was cleaned, ready for the next day, and the revenue handled carefully. If I had not gone on to college, I might be baking gourmet pizzas!

Your skills and talents in the workplace can change lives and change society. Fortunately for me, I did not quit learning and developing my abilities back in the pizza parlor. I know God's plan is that I always be a learner. The best approach to learning is to see it as a way of life.

• *Learning as a Way of Life*

My mother taught my sister and me to sew when we were in junior high. Later, the three of us would gather in the basement of our house and have a "sewingthon." I did take homemaking in college, but I first learned to sew from my mother.

You may not realize how many things you have learned and the many training experiences you have had in life. Take a minute and list things that someone has shown you how to do. Not long ago, I was waiting to get on an airplane when a retired Navy officer commented on the way I had tied my scarf. He was sure I had been in the military to have that "nice square knot." I had not been in the military, but I was in Girl Scouts. Learning to tie a square knot was just a part of being a Girl Scout. I cannot tell you how many times I have tied scarves, ribbons, and sashes for my friends because I can tie a nice square bow.

God intended for us to have teachable spirits. He gave us minds that can expand and gain more information and experience. A Bible study of the word *teach* reveals an expected way of life that is a learning life. God's plan for learning is not just in a classroom but also through experiences that come our way, through our successes and our failures, through our friends and family, and through God Himself. God's promise is that He will be the Teacher in our lives. He anticipates a willing response. Read His word for us from Psalm 32:

"I will instruct you and teach you
    in the way which you should go;
I will counsel you with My eye upon you.
Do not be as the horse or as the mule
    which have no understanding,
Whose trappings include bit and bridle to hold them in check,
Otherwise they will not come near to you."
    (Psalm 32:8 NASB)

Psalm 32:8 records God's promise to teach us with wise instruction. The Hebrew word for *teach* in Psalm 32:8 is *yara,* which has as its base meaning *to throw, shoot.* The word gives a sense of purpose to learning. God teaches us with a purpose that the talents and skills He has placed in our lives might be all that they can be to bless us so we can then bless others.

You may be that one in a million who instinctively knows all of God's plans for your life, but most of us learn from Him in other ways. He uses our homes to teach us. He uses our workplaces to teach us. He opens doors to management training, welding school, ceramics classes, or a college degree. He places in our hands the latest book on parenting, communication, or managing conflict. He dials the phone when the call comes to offer a soccer coaching job, a place on the school board, or a volunteer position at the local retirement center. The interesting fact about God is that He knows exactly what is needed to grow and develop the talents He has given us. He knows exactly what skills need to be developed for our life plans. What a great Teacher we have. Nothing is left to chance when He is the instructor.

Think again about the things you have learned in life. As you do, praise God for His wonderful teaching in your life.

Eating with a fork, using a potty, tying your shoes,
Talking, reading, writing, jumping jacks,
Marbles, spelling, math, drawing, singing, baseball,
Riding a bike, getting a gum ball, playing hide and seek,
Completing a form, driving, going to the store,
Using the phone, telling time,
Praying.

Now take a closer look at your personal learning journey. What unique things have you learned along the way? I listed things I learned to do. Celebrate with God the unique ways He has taught you.

Riding a horse, baking bread,
Flying an airplane, playing an instrument,
Sewing, painting, rocking a baby, acting, storying,
Cleaning a wound, making candles, sculpting, typing,
Accounting, investing, teaching, speaking,
Cleaning, repairing cars, fishing, skiing
Hiking, doing woodwork, listening,
Praying.

In the midst of all that we learn are those things God has enabled us to do that give us a sense of fulfillment and of value. What are those things in your life? What causes you to say, "I feel God's pleasure"? I feel His pleasure when I sing. I feel His pleasure when I bake an apple pie for a friend. I feel His pleasure when I invite my Chinese neighbors over for tea. I feel His pleasure when I take time to write a thank-you note. I feel His pleasure when I am telling another person about Jesus. I feel His pleasure when I leave my comfort zone to touch another life.

Talents and skills depend on use and training for continued worth. Even virtuosos are committed to practice and study their art. The more you use your most valuable abilities, the more effective you will become, and the greater will be your awareness of the person God created you to be.

❧ Learning Through Hobbies

A dear friend had a room full of unfinished projects for many years. She enjoyed a variety of activities and wanted to try everything. For her, the trying was the fun. Her hobby was not any particular project, but the fun of trying new things.

Hobbies are a terrific approach to trying something new or sharpening what you already do. One of my co-workers goes to a ceramics class each week to work off the stress of the day. Thanks to her hobby, I have some beautiful professional ceramic pieces in my home. Another co-worker does cross-stitching and "gifts" persons with works of art. When my daughter got married, a friend offered to do the flowers for her wedding because it was her hobby. Another friend directs weddings and plays golf for fun. I learned to make beeswax candles and enjoy both giving candles away and sometimes selling a pair.

When we become involved in a hobby, we sometimes discover natural abilities that may grow to become more than hobbies. My friend Marti enjoys going to garage sales and flea markets. She began to collect a few things. Her collection grew to the extent that she rented a small space in a large antique mall. The space did so well that she expanded into other shops. When the opportunity to sell online came along, she naturally expanded into the Internet arena. Even thought Marti is into flea markets for the fun of it, she has taken time to learn about the items she collects. Her growing knowledge base enabled her to purchase items for a couple of dollars and sell them for much more. Someday she will be doing all the time what she now does for fun.

We have a tendency in our busy lives to think we cannot pursue hobbies, but giving our minds a break from the stress of home and work makes us more creative people. Studies have shown that creativity is increased when we rest and when we break out of routine. Creativity is important for people created in God's image because our God is a creative God. Danny Cox writes in *Seize the Day* that "creative people tend to have a more light-hearted perspective on life because they can rise about the rat race and see the humor in most situations." God uses creativity to help move our lives from the ordinary to the extraordinary.

Hobbies can also be tools for touching lives around us. One group of women volunteered in an inner-city shelter for homeless women. One woman's hobby was crafts. Each month she brought a new craft to the shelter for the women to do with their children. Another woman gave beautifully smocked baby dresses to new single mothers. Women in poverty living in the Appalachian Mountains learned to quilt from a woman who did it as her hobby, but for them it became a way for feeding their families.

Learn to do something that adds beauty to your life, something that you can share with others or give away. Hobbies are another gift from God, given to us as a blessing so that we might bless others.

❧ *Looking for Signs of Success*

How do you know which talents and skills are most valuable in your life? The answer seems so simple, and yet persons often wander through the years never really sure of what they should be doing with their lives.

Eric Liddell's talent as a runner was such that he made the Olympic team for Great Britain in 1924. How did he know that he could run? Simple—he was successful at it. He won meet after meet. *The Flying Scotsman* describes Liddell's wild style saying "his arms were waving around like windmills. He attacked the air, he clawed the air, he punched the air. His chin was up, his head was so far back he seemed to be gazing at the sky. He wobbled a bit as he ran, too. But that extraordinary style propelled him toward the finishing tape faster than anyone else in the world. And the exhilaration on his face as he ran! The exultation on his face as he threw back his head! People never forgot their first sight of Eric Liddell running at full stretch" (from *The Flying Scotsman* by Sally Magnusson). Success is certainly an indicator that we are pursuing the right talents and skills.

Heather Whitestone is deaf. Against all odds she learned to speak and is seen in ads on television. When she competed for Miss Alabama and then Miss America, many thought she would not succeed. Heather knew she was to try for this honor and each success has confirmed what she thought God was leading her to do.

Running for Eric Liddell came easily, but learning to speak and to communicate in a hearing world was not easy for Heather. The ease with which a talent is perfected or a skill is learned is not so much an indicator of its value to us as the results when it is used. Remember that God knows our talents and skills. He is the one who turns an ordinary ability into an extraordinary craft.

Voices are always ready to tell us we will fail. The world would often keep us from trying. If we change the channel so we hear only the voice of our Father, the problems the world puts before us become mere challenges, and challenges are motivating influences. The talent that seemed weak, or the skill that seemed impossible to learn, may be the very thing that God wants to use. At one point in the movie *Mission Impossible 2*, hero Ethan Hunt is concerned about a job he is assigned. His boss, Mr. Phelps, explains that the job is difficult, but not impossible. Therefore, it can be done. Difficult is nothing for the God of the extraordinary.

≥ *Improving our Skills and Talents*

You have already seen many stories of women using and improving their abilities. I am still concerned that every woman know and use the tools for life that God has placed in her hands. God has given us everything we need to live the abundant life. Since this is a reality, why are so many women continuing to feel valueless, useless, bored, and undirected? Why are so many needs in our homes, our communities, and the world going unmet? Could it be that many of us are afraid to claim the wondrous truth of God's good gifts to us? In case you are still struggling with this issue in any area of your life, here is a list of means you can use to explore and develop your creativity.

• Play with children.
• Take a class to learn a craft.
• Learn to play a computer game.
• Make your own greeting card for a friend.
• Change vocations.
• Wrap all your gifts in a unique look that is just you.
• Choose someone who needs affirmation and give them a small gift every day.
• See how many people you can smile at in a day.
• Begin walking every day.
• Take a different route to work or to church.
• Volunteer for new responsibilities at church, a club, or at work.
• Begin working on a college degree.
• Take a short vacation to somewhere you have never been.
• Go shopping in a different part of town.
• Make a new friend.
• Ask friends to tell you what you do well.
• Change something in your house.
• Try a ministry in your community that you think you cannot do.
• Listen for times when people say you have done a good job.
• Be aware of God's presence and "feel His pleasure."

Jerry Flack offers several strategies for developing talents in his book, *TalentEd, Strategies for Developing the Talent in Every Learner*. I listed a few of these here and reworked a few for our purposes to encourage you even further to take a big leap into extraordinary living.

• Read books and increase your vocabulary.
• Write your own biography and read the biographies of others.

- Make your own catalogs with pictures and descriptions of things you want to do and places you want to see.
- Daydream and share your dreams with others.
- Begin a new business, such as selling homemade jelly or making beeswax candles.
- Write a story based on what you would like to see happen in your life.
- Participate in a drama.
- Write a letter to yourself expressing your hope for the future.
- Keep a journal of everything you learn and try.
- Imagine you are participating in a mystery and begin looking for clues in your life about the future.
- Read the newspaper and evaluate what you read, looking for ways you can get involved and change situations in your community.
- Participate in a new sport.
- Ask persons questions about the work they do, what they like, what they do not like, and the skills they use.
- Make up your own recipes.
- Find ways to serve others.
- Do not turn on the television for a week and learn something new during that time.
- Learn to write poetry.
- Look up words you do not know in the dictionary and use them.
- Read articles in encyclopedias and resources.
- Become an expert on a specific subject, such as a particular type of dog, cat, plant, etc.

Eric Liddell was not only a great athlete, but he was also a great Christian. At a memorial after his death, one of the ministers who had known him since childhood said, "From my knowledge of him, gained in this close association over many years, I say that Eric is the most remarkable example in my experience of a man of average ability and talents developing those talents to an amazing degree, and even appearing to acquire new talents from time to time, through the power of the Holy Spirit. He was, literally, God-controlled, in his thought, judgement, actions, words, to an extent I have never seen surpassed, and rarely seen equaled."

Chapter Five

Heavenly Gifts

Unity, call, service and love,
Spiritual ribbons from heaven above,
Wrap spiritual gifts for a spiritual birth,
A lavish gift-giving from heaven to earth.
A sky full of angels, all waiting to see,
What I will do
With God's good gifts to me!

The evening began like any other, but it became an unforgettable moment. Twelve women gathered to study a book
on spiritual gifts. I had not given spiritual gifts much
thought. If you had asked me, "What spiritual gifts have you
seen in your life?" I would have stuttered in denial. The study

went as a study usually does until the end. One by one we went around the room, taking time to affirm spiritual gifts we had seen exhibited in the life of each woman there. I remember a moment of fear. What if they had not seen any in my life? Then, over and over, they said to me, "You have the gift of *faith*." One evening and one word became more important in my journey than winning the lottery or achieving fame.

You are blessed with every spiritual blessing through Jesus Christ. At the moment of your spiritual birth, you were blessed with gifts that God intends for you to use. He *lavished* on you gifts that enable you to be the instrument of the Holy Spirit "for the common good" as 1 Corinthians 12:7 clearly states.

Christian humility does not call for a denial of our giftedness. The opposite is true. Since our gifts are a blessing from God, we are claiming nothing we have done in ourselves but gifts freely and divinely given. God is glorified when we acknowledge the gifts He has given to us. To deny His gracious gift-giving is to deny His Word. Celebrate God's gifts in your life by appreciating and using them in your interaction with others.

Discovering your spiritual gifts is an adventure. Just as understanding the depth of God's Word takes time in study and prayer, so discovering our God-given gifts takes the discipline of obedience and service. The gifts God has given you will never be exhausted or grow old. Rather, the more you use them and bestow them on others through service, the more abundant they become.

❧ Talents Need Spiritual Gifts

I mentioned my friend Marti who loves flea markets. While she has a real talent for finding bargains that are worth far more than she invested and a good memory that is helping her to excel as a dealer, she is also a Christian. She cares about people and takes time to build relationships, which opens doors to sharing her faith in Christ. Her talent is made extraordinary by her spiritual gift of evangelism.

Everyone has talents. Spiritual gifts, on the other hand, are only given to Christians. According to Stuart Calvert, in her book *Uniquely Gifted,* spiritual gifts are given to us at the time of our conversion. Spiritual gifts are developed through the power of the Holy Spirit. Spiritual gifts are God at work in you as you consecrate your talents to God's service. This is well explained by the apostle Paul to the Christians at Corinth.

"Now concerning spiritual gifts, brothers and sisters, I do not want you to be uninformed. Now there are varieties of gifts, but the same Spirit; and there are varieties of services, but the same Lord; and there are varieties of activities, but it is the same God who activates all of them in everyone. To each is given the manifestation of the Spirit for the common good." (1 Cor. 12:1, 4–7)

God wants to bring all aspects of our lives together for the good of those around us. God acts extraordinarily through us when we allow Him to take our talents, activities, and services and empower them with the spiritual gifts that come to all His children.

ಶ Spiritual Gifts Need Spiritual Fruits

A recent article gave an account of a young woman who is well known for her spiritual gifts of knowledge and teaching. The article mentioned that the members of her church acknowledge that she lives what she teaches. In other words, she is rich in spiritual fruits, God's character; this Christlikeness enables her to teach with authority. Those who hear her trust her teaching because she reflects Christ. What a powerful affirmation for any one of us to receive. Spiritual gifts *increase the value* of your natural abilities and talents. On the other hand, spiritual gifts *have little value* without the spiritual fruits that reveal Christ in you.

The gifts that God has given you come alive when God's character is the driving force behind your service. Think back to the chapter on personality and the wholeness that comes from taking on God's character, those spiritual fruits listed in Galatians 5:22–23. Imagine what can happen when a Sympathetic has the spiritual fruit of gentleness and is using the spiritual gift of teaching. Her compassion will radiate from her eyes and words, and those who are learning from her will seek to have the same compassion they see in their teacher. She becomes a mentor, teaching through her life more than words could ever say.

❧ *Extraordinary Blessings of Spiritual Gifts*

You may remember Miss Havisham in *Great Expectations*. She was left standing at the altar. She then left the wedding feast untouched for years following that heartbreaking experience. She even left the wedding gifts unopened.

God wants you to open the gifts He has given you. Each gift has been designed to bless you and to provide you with just what you need to the live life to the fullest. Not only that, you will discover that as your gifts are opened, you will long to share them with others. The gifts God gave you as a blessing become blessings to others.

Notice that last statement. *The gifts God gave you as a blessing become blessings to others.* Wrapped around the spiritual gifts God gives are four important ribbons that have to do with blessing us and blessing others. The first ribbon is God's call or the intention that He gives to our lives, the reason for giving us His gifts. The second ribbon is unity that comes as we work together using our various spiritual gifts to achieve His purposes. The third ribbon is service. Spiritual gifts are used to serve others. The fourth ribbon is love, the only right motivation for using our gifts in service and the absolute requirement for unity. Before looking at the individual gifts, let's think about these ribbons that make our spiritual gifts extraordinarily beautiful.

The Beautiful Ribbon of God's Call

Spiritual gifts are linked to the call that God has on our lives. The gifts passage in Ephesians 4 begins by reminding God's people to *"lead a life worthy of the calling"* to which they have been called. The gifts passage in Romans 12 begins by encouraging the reader to do the will of God. The gifts passage in 1 Corinthians 12 reminds Christians that they have been called to a new way of life and are to turn away from their past pagan ways. 1 Peter 4:2 also calls Christians to live *"no longer by human desires but by the will of God."*

Spiritual gifts are given to enable us to fulfill God's plan for our lives. When we do not use our gifts, we cannot fulfill our God-given destiny. We limit the possibility of living with a sense of purpose and satisfaction. Many Christians go through life wondering what life is really all about because they never grasp the truth that they are gifted for God's plan for their lives. God gives us spiritual gifts to enable us to live the extraordinary life.

The Beautiful Ribbon of Unity

I was invited to travel through one of our states and visit the women's ministry leadership teams in several churches. Each team told me how they were meeting the needs of the women in their church. They acknowledged the value of the gifts that each leader had to offer. I met women with gifts of teaching, ministry, missions, evangelism, prayer, hospitality, service, etc. The women on these leadership teams affirmed working together to

Heavenly Gifts

accomplish what one could not do alone. They affirmed the value of one another's gifts.

Each individual gift is important to God's kingdom, and no gift is complete apart from the gifts of others. After all, we are reborn into a family, and we really do need each other.

The fact that we are united does not diminish our individual uniqueness. To the contrary, our unity complements our uniqueness. For instance, the leg without a foot is still a leg, but it is less effective in its God-designed role. When the foot is added, the leg can dance, run, walk, balance, and on and on. Likewise, the foot needs the leg to function at all. Each of these body parts is unique. When they function in harmony, they are incredible.

Stuart Calvert writes in *Uniquely Gifted:* "The body of Christ is composed of people with many abilities, enabling them to minister in a variety of ways. The Holy Spirit blends our differences into a unique unity without stereotyping individuals. He preserves the individuality of personalities . . . In the body of Christ, one richly endowed believer cannot be and do everything. All members, harmonizing a diversity of impressive or inconspicuous gifts, cause the body to function properly. An attempt to stereotype members of the body conflicts with the good, acceptable, perfect will of God."

The Beautiful Ribbon of Service
Service is a *learned* response to life, but Christians have an advantage in that we have been uniquely equipped for serving. Have you watched Tim the Tool Man on *Home Improvement?* He wears a tool apron filled with tools needed for home improvement projects. *You* have a tool apron, also. Your tools are spiritual gifts, and they are just what you need to serve.

The Bible makes clear that spiritual gifts are not to be a source of pride but an avenue of service. That's right. Your spiritual gifts are given to you for service. The Christians in Asia Minor, Corinth, Ephesus, and Rome were slow to understand that spiritual gifts made them servants rather than kings. As we discovered in Chapter Two, service is an extraordinary way to live.

The Beautiful Ribbon of Love

Paul declares love as the *composer* of the Christian life. He makes clear that spiritual gifts apart from love are like cheap noisemakers to a symphony. Exercise your spiritual gift for any reason other than love and you will soon become discouraged. The emphasis is clear. Do not teach without love. Do not help in the church kitchen without love. Do not lead a group without love. Do not tell others about Jesus without love. Do not serve without love. You are wasting your time. Love is the governing rule for every act of service.

Imagine you are at a birthday party—your party. You have been lavished with gifts, and they are piled high on the table. Each gift has four beautiful ribbons tied around it. You untie each of the four ribbons and open the gift. Immediately you are aware of God's call in your life. You sense a new unity with your Christian sisters and brothers. You cannot wait to go with them to serve and touch other lives. Above all, the love you feel for others splashes over onto everyone around you. This is the wonder of God's lavish gift-giving.

❧ God's Lavish Gift-Giving

Our granddaughter Chelsea informed us that she was having a Cinderella birthday when she turned four. For the entire year, she talked about her Cinderella birthday. She told her parents, grandparents, and great-grandparents. What kind of birthday do you think she had? You guessed it. She had a Cinderella birthday. She had a Cinderella dress, tiara, shoes, games, decorations, and a Cinderella cake to top it off. Needless to say, lavishing these gifts on her brought our family great joy. Even so, the joy we felt does not compare with the joy of our heavenly Father "who has blessed us in Christ with every spiritual blessing in the heavenly places" (Eph. 1:3b).

Most theologians agree that the spiritual gifts mentioned in the New Testament are not exhaustive lists. In fact, each list is different. Since God is the provider, He may well provide spiritual gifts as needed in each local body of believers, as well as for each situation and each generation of believers. The spiritual gifts that you discovered in your personal experience may not even be mentioned in the Scriptures. Is this hard to believe when we consider the resources of God?

The apostle Paul's lists of spiritual gifts include apostleship, prophecy, teaching, ministry, evangelism, exhortation, giving, compassion, forms of assistance, various kinds of leadership, wisdom, knowledge, faith, hospitality, healing, working of miracles, discernment of spirits, tongues, and interpretation of tongues. The apostle Peter mentions speaking and serving as representative of all the gifts.

Every gift you have is evidence that you have been "marked with the seal of the promised Holy Spirit" (Eph. 1:13). If you have ever felt like an ordinary woman, realize now that as a Christian, in whom the Holy Spirit dwells, nothing about you is ordinary. Many gifts are available from God, and some of these are yours. Do you know yet what they are?

The Gift of Apostleship

Paul lists first the gift of apostleship. This gift is characterized in the life of the apostles in the New Testament. These men had first-hand experience with Jesus. They were called to take the gospel to the world. Today, many describe the gift that missionaries receive as the gift of apostleship. The apostle is called to serve beyond the local church. You may serve as a leader who provides training and services to several churches in the area. You may serve as an elected officer for the churches in your state. You may feel a responsibility to help other churches develop their leaders and their ministries. You may be called to serve as a volunteer on a regular basis, going to other places to meet needs and share Christ. You may travel with ease to places you have never been. These are possible evidences of the gift of apostleship. Reaching beyond the local community is still a responsibility for today's church. If you have the gift of apostleship, you can assist others to risk beyond the familiar environment.

The Gift of Prophecy

Paul also mentions the gift of prophecy. Prophets are bold in applying the Word of God to the social and moral issues of the day. They have a unique ability to call God's people to repentance and revival. They are servants of the Word and are able to build up the church as they speak with authority the intention of God.

The woman with the gift of prophecy is able to clearly speak the truths of God in such a way as to encourage and strengthen the church. You may have the gift of prophecy if you tend to speak out to warn that Christian principles apply to all aspects of life or if you confront injustice with authority. If so, become an advocate to guide women toward godly lives.

Study the lives and messages of the Old Testament prophets. What was their message and how did they present it? Participate in a small group where you can learn to speak God's truths to impact lives. Gain knowledge concerning biblical truths. If asked to speak before a group or church, let God reveal His power to call His people to commitment through your gift of prophecy.

The Gift of Teaching

Another gift is that of teaching. The gifted teacher has the ability to share Bible truths in such a way that hearers can apply the Bible to their daily lives. Jesus was called Teacher. He used every situation as a teachable moment. He revealed the truths of God through illustrations from the ordinary events of life. Your desire to study and interpret God's Word and the ability to take the complexities of Scripture and bring them into the context of today's world may be the gift of teaching in you. If so, everyday events are your prize opportunities to bring a biblical truth to life. Teachers who use their gift can change the lives of children in a public school, create a climate where persons can respond to Christ, and help individuals to see how God's Word is applicable in the situations they encounter.

The Gift of Ministry
The dynamic gift of ministry propels the Christian into exciting ventures of caring for those who cannot help themselves. The hungry, the poor, the wealthy, the lonely, the imprisoned, the forgotten, the young, the old, and the sick are the recipients of the gracious caring gift of ministry. Ministry is the gift that softens a heart to hear the gospel. Ministry is the visible sign of God's love to a lost and hurting world. Your desire to be personally engaged in changing the world around you may be the gift of ministry at work in your spirit. If you have the gift of ministry, God will use your skills to lift persons out of hopelessness into God's grace. If you know of a need, try to meet it. God will give you the resources you need as you obey His prompting.

The Gift of Evangelism
Ministry creates an environment for evangelism. Those who have the gift of evangelism have a deep burden for the lost, a persistent sense of urgency to spread the gospel, and a bold approach to verbal expression of their faith in Christ. Is it easy for you to bring the name of Jesus into a conversation? Are you quick to notice the opportunity to share your faith? You may have the gift of evangelism. If so, begin in your home a group to reach non-Christians. Participate in the church visitation program. Spend time developing relationships with persons who

may not have had life-changing encounter with Christ. Learn the skills for accurately presenting the gospel. You will find that leading another to Christ motivates you to do it again and again.

The Gift of Exhortation

The gift of exhortation reminds me of Barnabas, who encouraged Paul when he was a new Christian. Barnabas stood by Paul when other Christians doubted his conversion. An exhorter is one to whom you can turn when your heart is hurting. The gift of exhortation brings to the church just what it needs to hold on in faith when the going is rough. You may have the gift of exhortation. If so, you find great joy in bringing comfort and strength to those who need to know that someone cares. Exhorters have a ready supply of encouraging words or other expressions of support. They are good listeners. They know when and what to say to help the discouraged face the world and its obstacles. Exhorters send letters to missionaries, give hugs, smile, listen, and express God's love to those who are down. Is this your gift?

The Gift of Giving

All of these fairly visible gifts are no more important than those that are less conspicuous, such as the gift of giving. Giving is basic to meeting the needs of the world. People with the gift of giving base their life decisions on what they can give rather than what they can receive. Individual material resources do not determine the presence of the gift of giving. You may recall the woman Jesus saw give her offering in the temple. He said she gave more than the rich did because she gave all she had. All she had was a mite. A person with the gift of giving releases her dominance of her money and possessions, never considering her openhandedness as a loss or a sacrifice. You may be a gifted giver. If this is so, the exercise of your gift greatly advances God's work.

The Gift of Compassion

The gift of compassion is also known as the gift of mercy. Compassion is the trademark of Jesus' ministry. He was moved with compassion by the suffering of the people. Such compassion is more than emotion. It is an active response to the needs of the world. Compassion enables an individual to empathize with another's suffering, to not pass judgment, to be a patient presence, and to relieve pain with caring words and actions. If you are drawn to those dying with AIDS, to the homeless mother struggling to raise her children, to the recovering drug addict, or to take the first step toward reconciliation with your enemy, you may have the gift of compassion. Compassion is the beacon of peace in our world.

The Gift of Helps

The gift of helps finds expression in the supporting activities carried on behind the scenes. People with the gift of helps do those important jobs that keep the church open and stimulate fellowship among the family of God. People working in the kitchen, doing yard work, organizing the church library, cleaning the sanctuary, repairing the plumbing, or driving the church van are just a few ways we see the gift of helps in motion. Do you prefer to go about quietly taking care of those things that often go unnoticed by others? Are you the one who picks up hymnals abandoned on the church floor? Do you stay to make sure the church kitchen and fellowship hall are sparkling clean? You have the gift of helps. Without you the doors of many church buildings would close.

The Gift of Leadership

Leadership, a misunderstood but important gift, looks for a place of service rather than authority. Leaders are efficient at guiding the church to make decisions, accomplish goals, and develop the potential of all members. In fact, leaders are the ones who help persons discover and use their gifts. A woman with the gift of leadership provides an example of Christlikeness that encourages others to follow. If you enjoy setting and achieving goals, helping others to do the same, and bringing together all types of people with all kinds of gifts to work together toward a goal, then you have some clear signs of the gift of leadership.

The Gifts of Wisdom and Knowledge

Wisdom and knowledge work hand in hand. Together, these gifts clarify the direction to take as we seek to fulfill God' comprehensive design for our lives.

According to Stuart Calvert, the gift of wisdom allows an individual to handle her emotional involvement, listen to all opinions, and suggest a solution. Has your experience as a Christian revealed an unusual ability to make the right decision and to help others make wise decisions? Are you able to look at complex information and see a clear solution? Welcome to the gift of wisdom. Be sure you are present at church business meetings. Be aware that you may be able to bring about peaceful resolution to situations that are potentially disruptive.

On the other hand, the gift of knowledge is the divine capacity for learning. When you have the gift of knowledge, you know where to find answers and how to arrange the information so it is useful for making decisions. You know how to look for answers in the Bible and can provide the information needed as the church makes decisions about growth, ministries, worship approaches, and resources to use. Can you think of any incidences in your church in which people with the gifts of knowledge and wisdom helped your church or women's group to make a critical decision? What providential care our Heavenly Father has conferred upon us!

The Gift of Faith

Faith is revealed in actions that demonstrate confidence or trust in God. Without the gift of faith, churches would miss opportunities to extend their ministries in directions they would never have considered on their own. A woman of faith trusts God in every circumstance. A woman of faith is certain of God's will for her life. She allows Him to take her hand each day and lead her into service. Can you rate your faith quotient on a scale of 1 to 10? What actions demonstrate your faith? Women of faith are catalysts for churches choosing to send dozens of volunteers around the world, take on a ministry with parolees, or bring to church children whose parents have no interest in God. Can you name a person in your church who has the gift of faith?

The Gift of Hospitality

Everyone appreciates the person with the gift of hospitality. A person with this gift can make anyone and everyone feel at home and welcome. The gift of hospitality does not rely on expensive furnishings or a perfectly clean home. A woman with the gift of hospitality enjoys providing for the comfort of others. Youth choirs, visiting missionaries, lonely neighbors are all recipients of the fruits that result when a woman uses her gift of hospitality. You can be sure you have the gift of hospitality if a house full of happy people is your favorite way of living.

The Gift of Discernment

According to Stuart Calvert in *Uniquely Gifted* another important gift, discernment, enables one to "detect deficiency in the truth of a sermon, a book, a speech, or a conversation." A discerner may spot a phony and protect the church from being led astray by a "false Christ." The gift of discernment carries with it great accountability because you can see beyond words and actions to the heart and mind.

The Gifts of Healing and Miracles

The last gifts Paul mentioned often inspire intense debates. Two of these gifts are healing and miracles. Medical doctors and science in general certainly confirm that divine healing takes place today. Stories of miracles are in the news every day. Yet theologians argue without finality over the presence of these gifts in today's world. The gifts of healing and miracles existed in biblical times. Therefore God remains sovereign over their use through the church today.

The Gifts of Tongues and Interpretation of Tongues

The last gifts are tongues and interpretation of tongues. Paul provides a lengthy discussion of these in 1 Corinthians 14. According to Paul, one with the gift of tongues should exercise this gift in the church only when someone with the gift of interpretation is also present. Paul suggested that these gifts be used with caution for the church is edified and strengthened only when members understand what is being said.

⅔ *Gifted for Extraordinary Living*

Now that you have read through the above gifts, go back to each gift and evaluate for yourself how much you see this gift in your life. Sometimes you will see that you have a gift but you are not using it as you could and should. Perhaps God is opening a door for you to use the gift you have, but you have resisted. Is it time to reconsider? Your heavenly Father wants to bless you. Will you let Him have His way? His gift-giving is all about extraordinary living.

Chapter Six

Life-Changing Experience

Yesterday, today, and tomorrow,
Already lived, living now, and yet to live,
Promise found, lost, and found again.
Are some days to be remembered and others not?
Or is there some redeeming love
In every day that Christ has bought?

Nine women stood before the crowd of a thousand or more. We could see only their backs until they turned to face us. Each woman held an enlarged photo, a mug shot, a photo taken at her last arrest, the person she used to be. What a transformation had taken place! We were in awe of their beauty and poise as they told their stories of alcohol and crack cocaine addiction, life as a stripper, abuse, jail time, prostitution—and Jesus Christ. Christ bought their days of failure and turned those days to the praise of God's glory. These women had no need to hide their experiences. God embraced every moment of their lives with His love. Their stories were now God's story with no need for shame or guilt.

What is your story? How much of it is still hidden in a closet? How much of your story still waits for God's transforming grace? When I was a girl, I took some candy from a store without paying for it. I did not tell anyone what I had done. When confronted, I tried to lie my way out of the situation. When I think back on that experience, I am well aware that what I did was not pleasing to God. I had a dark experience that I wanted to hide from my mother and anyone else who would recognize what I had done for what it was.

Some experiences in my life have been the kind that I wanted to keep hidden. I did not want anyone to know that I had failed or that I had lived in a way that was unworthy. Yet I have found that every time I open my experiences to God's forgiveness, I discover anew that nothing is more freeing than being honest about who I am before God. I can position every experience within the forgiveness of God offered in Jesus Christ and begin anew.

All of life's experiences can become tools for our good through Christ. He has much to teach us. With His encouragement and forgiveness, our experiences will help us to see just how great our God is and how great is His love for us.

❧ Knowledge and Values

Experience broadens the knowledge on which we base our values. Consider this story from the Old Testament.

David saw her across the way, bathing. He could not resist her beauty and sent his servants to bring her to him. So began

David's affair with Bathsheba, which led to the death of her husband. The prophet Nathan confronted David with his sin, and David fell on his face in fasting and prayer. Even so, David paid dearly, losing the son that Bathsheba gave him, seeing his family and his kingdom torn apart, and losing his position as king.

David learned that God does not tolerate adultery or murder. Even a king is not free to set standards that differ from the laws of God. As I read the psalms of David and the chapters that tell of his life after his experience with Bathsheba, I see a man humbled, one who learned the hard way what sin can do in a life. Sadly, David's experience was the kind that rips lives apart to such an extent that it takes generations to put them back together again. Fortunately, not every experience through which we learn our values is so completely destructive to those around us.

The joy of this story is that the Lord never stopped loving David. The Lord wanted David to understand and know Him better, and He did not let David get away with murder and adultery. The Lord wanted David to understand the value that He places on honesty, life, and fidelity. Do you think David's value base was changed for the better? I do. Even though he had to deal with the consequences, I believe he chose God's way and God's values.

Earlier in this chapter, I mentioned stealing candy as a child. When I look back to that time, I remember the embarrassment of getting caught, the heartbreak in my mother's eyes, and the punishment that followed. I am convinced that stealing was not a good choice to make. I recall how cheapened I was in my own eyes and how much I harmed others. That experience and others have taught me such values as honesty, forgiveness, integrity, consistency, dependability, and many other values that I want to exhibit in my life.

Christian growth depends on experiences that enable us to confirm for ourselves the truths we have been taught as children. Perhaps our parents told us it is wrong to steal or wrong to kill.

Such values can only become ours as we question them for ourselves through Bible study and prayer.

Fortunately, we do not have to steal, murder, lie, or cheat to know that these are not God's values. Study of God's Word and review of our world provide all the evidence needed to prove that God's values are the only values that really work. Disrupted homes, serious illness, death, prison, poverty, loss of esteem, failing economies, and many other situations reveal the truth that only God's values bring life and love to people who struggle to find meaningful existence in today's world.

Some time ago I attended a study on world hunger. The material we used explained the reasons for and the effects of hunger on peoples around the world. My past experience with hunger was limited, but through this study my eyes were opened to the value God places on human life. When I arrived home from the study, I felt God leading me to care about hungry people. As a result, I changed my eating habits and my giving habits. I participated in ministries that helped hungry people.

Since values are the foundation on which we base many of our decisions, experience helps cement God's values as the underpinning for all we do. What experiences have taught you God's values? Are you staying true to those values? Choose experiences that will reinforce what you have already discovered about a godly value system. Allow God to show you the experiences that He has prepared just for you.

❧ New Ideas and Possibilities

When my daughter was in middle school, I attended a major training event for children's Bible teachers. My experience up to that point had given me limited contact with women who served in vocational ministry. At the training event, I met seminary-trained women who served as ministers in their churches, working with preschoolers and children. I was stirred in my heart to see how God had gifted these women and was using them in his service.

Until this experience, I thought my place of ministry would always be as a volunteer through my church. I had not considered that I could serve God in a vocational ministry. When I arrived home, I shared my thoughts of possible future ministry with my husband and friends. The questions in my mind were numerous. Not only did I not have a seminary degree, I did not even have a college degree. I did not live where I could work toward one. The practical aspects were completely out of sync with the call I sensed in my heart.

I believe God used that experience to open my eyes to the possibilities and to prepare me for the next step in His plan for my life. He was already at work in ways I did not know. A few months later, I received a letter offering me a position with our state denominational office. I was sure I could not do this, but God overcame every barrier and doubt to achieve His plan for my life. Most amazing of all is that I found myself in college. I completed my college degree and went on to seminary. The possibilities that had challenged me at the Bible teacher's training became realities.

Experience leads to new ideas and possibilities. Be where God wants you to be when He wants you there. He has great plans for you that you may never consider if you do not have the experience that He has planned for you. Be alert to the ideas He shows you, for His plans are always extraordinary.

❧ Sense of Intuition

Great leaders have learned to listen to and trust their intuitive side. For those of us who know Christ, I am convinced that trusting the intuitive element of our humanity becomes ever more valuable as God surprises us with opportunities to touch the world around us.

A few years ago my mother and father were traveling in Maine when my father became ill. A trip to the doctor revealed cancer, but the extent and seriousness of the cancer was being thoroughly checked by the doctors. My parents were waiting to get the results. They assured me that they were fine, but I knew that I had to be there with them. I flew to Maine, and together we waited for the doctors' reports.

The report was not good: untreatable cancer, a few months at best, no known cure, no known treatment that was of any value. The shocking words took our breath away. I think back to that moment often, wishing I could change the doctor's words. Even so, I was right where I needed to be at one of the most difficult times in my family's life. Fortunately, I had learned to trust my inner voice that told me what I needed to do at that time.

The Bible does not speak of intuition, but many stories cause me to wonder if God's people acted in response to the godly nurturing of their inner voices. How did God speak to Abraham to lead him to a distant country? How was it that Rebekah knew that it was good to go with Isaac and become his wife? How did Jesus' first followers know following this unknown man was right? Did these people respond to the discomfort that comes when we sense that we are to speak or act in a certain way? I tend to believe that Barnabas was an intuitive man. He somehow knew that Saul could be trusted (Acts 9:27), and later he knew that John Mark was a person of value to God (Acts 15:36–39). When we take on the mind of Christ, our thoughts, motives, and urgings are more likely to reflect His knowledge of the situations we face and His plan for our lives.

Trusting our intuitive side is easier each time we discover through experience that we can depend on the inner voice. The most confident adults I know are those whose experience has equipped them to trust their intuition enough to move ahead on the decisions they make. Most experiences require some amount of intuitive judgment, for we can never really know all there is to know about a subject or situation. We can do our best to gather the facts, but at some point we will have to act on whatever knowledge is available to us at the moment.

The inner voice is a God-given part of who we are and worthy of our attention when it pricks at our hearts or minds. Experience teaches us to depend on God and stay closely connected to Him so we can know that the inner voice is also His gentle whisper. In the moments that we have to make decisions without time to think or take action with limited knowledge, we are more secure in the outcome when we have been listening to God and allowing Him to mold the intuitive side of who we are.

Experience develops our sense of intuition. Intuition helps us to see beyond the facts, and in some ways may be the tool God has given us to look into the future, take risks, and see what He has for us on the other side of this moment.

✐ ❧ Out of the Comfort Zone

A deep and heavy snow fell overnight, creating treacherous roads with ice, blowing snow, and snowdrifts. Even so, the group of women planning to go to a women's event decided they were willing to brave the conditions to make the five-hour drive. The two cars of determined women made it safely to their destination and enjoyed three days of worship, study, and fellowship. The fact that they were snowed in once they arrived did not dampen their enthusiasm or their openness to hear a word from the Lord.

A few years later, one of the women was traveling alone to attend another meeting across the state. After traveling a few hours, she ran into a major snowstorm of blizzard proportions. The roads were glazed with ice, and the snow was deep on either side. As she drove along the interstate, she saw a van slide into the center median and turn upside down. She pulled over, parked her car, and ran into the snow toward the van, fearing the worst for the passengers. When she arrived, she found a man, his son, and the family parakeet, physically okay but shaken. She helped them out of the van and took them to her car where they remained safe and warm until help came.

Another few years passed. This same woman was team leader for a group of 24 women and one man who were to take Bibles into Russia. The trip was almost canceled when two weeks before they were to go, tanks rolled through downtown Moscow, people were killed, and the situation became volatile. No one knew whether communism or freedom would win. The sponsoring mission agency called to tell the team members they would most likely have to cancel their trip.

When the team leader called group members and discovered their commitment to go, she told them to pray that God would open the doors. She believed it was God's plan for them to distribute Bibles in the Russian language, which for the first time could be done openly without fear of imprisonment. Three days before they were to leave, the sending agency called and said, "Go!" Her team, along with another team, distributed more than 70,000 Russian language New Testaments, led former communists and Muslims to Christ, and witnessed in Red Square, the Kremlin, orphanages, hospitals, prisons, hotels, and streets everywhere. From Moscow to Yalta on the Black Sea, to Kyrghisia, a Muslim state, the women shared their faith in Christ.

Each experience in this woman's life empowered her for the next adventure with Christ. A small step and then another small step makes each door that the Lord opens easier to approach. The experiences of a lifetime are all factors in making the most of opportunities we have. Since I travel by myself all over the nation and the world, many women ask how I am comfortable traveling alone. The truth of the matter is that God has shown He is faithful to care for me wherever I am, regardless of whether I am alone or with others.

For years, I traveled in the safe environment of my parents. Then I traveled with my husband in his work. When I was a young woman, I traveled with church friends to training events in other states. A few years later, I held a professional position that meant traveling by car across the state on a regular basis. Then I found myself in a national consulting role that meant I was traveling by air in and out of the US. The next step was being responsible for others as I took them with me into unknown territories and situations for the cause of Christ.

You have many experiences in your life that equip you to take God's hand when He invites you to go with Him into places where persons are hungering for hope. Note God's word to you as you step out into the unknown.

"I am the Lord, I have called you in righteousness, I have taken you by the hand and kept you; I have given you as a covenant to the people, a light to the nations, to open the eyes that are blind, to bring out the prisoners from the dungeon, from the prison those who sit in darkness." (Isa. 42:6–7)

The extraordinary life that God gives always leads us beyond our comfort zones. He wants us to see with our own eyes how He provides, how He empowers, and how He is faithful and sufficient in all things. Comfort zones keep us from relying on Him alone. Think of your comfort zones, the ones that may be keeping you from relying solely on God. Some of these are financial security, retirement plans, job certainty, family and friends, safety, and even our homes. Every item mentioned is good, but at some point the extraordinary life that God offers you may mean leaving any one of these pleasures behind to see what He will do. You are ready. The experiences of your lifetime prepared you for the next step with your heavenly Father.

❧ Acceptance and Empathy

When Moses' sister Miriam was struck with leprosy, I suspect that she was absolutely shocked. After all, she was the sister of the leader of all the Hebrews. She was as close to being aristocracy as possible among the Israelites fleeing from Egypt.

Have you had experiences in your life that make it clear that today may be a day of grace but tomorrow the boom may fall? My friend Rose always says, "Can't I read about this in a book?" when referring to the hard times we have to go through in life. The problem is that until we have been there ourselves, we can't always understand the emotional, spiritual, and even physical toll that difficult times extol on victims and family and friends.

When my friend's husband was in the last stages of cancer, I sat with him for an afternoon while she went out to the barn where they had enjoyed polishing rocks together for many years. She needed a short break from the heartache and stress of caring for the one she loved so much. Her husband was mildly aware of my presence and was sometimes fretful with pain and suffering. The cancer filled his body with fluid to the extent that it ran through his skin. He would kick his legs off the bed. When I lifted his leg to put it back on the bed, the blood and water would run through my fingers. Not until that experience did I understand the suffering that came with such an illness, both for him and for her.

About that same time, I volunteered in a preschool for special needs children. Each week I spent a morning assisting the teachers by spending time with children who suffered all types of physical and mental challenges. One boy showed little evidence of awareness. I sat with him, moving his legs and arms, talking to him, and giving him as much stimulation and body movement as I could. I often thought what it must be like to be the parent, responsible for the care day in and day out for a child so lovable and yet unable to respond.

Experiences open our eyes to the world of God's love and care. We think we understand, but then we find we are face to face with God's faithfulness in a whole new dimension.

Sandi Rives discovered a new depth of compassion through an experience she had with her Sunday morning Bible study class. Perhaps her story will encourage you to follow your inner voice and participate in new ministries outside your comfort zone but exactly where God wants to use you.

Sandi's Story

Our Sunday School Class became involved as an AIDS Care Team through the AIDS clinic at the university hospital in our city. The clinic was looking for individuals or groups willing to provide support for people with AIDS. It was not presented as a ministry, but our class determined it could be one. The clinic representatives stressed the intensity of the commitment. Frankly, some of us were concerned about how some in our class would respond to a person with AIDS, but not for long. One of the class members voiced the thoughts of the rest. "You don't think we would back away from this kind of ministry just because we don't approve of the lifestyle that got him in trouble, do you?"

We were the first class at our church to become an AIDS care team. It was a strange feeling to begin a ministry knowing that the person to whom we ministered would soon die. We had several training sessions with a staff member from the clinic. We learned what we could and could not do, and things we should do. The trainers encouraged us to not be afraid to touch our patient, including shaking hands and giving pats on the arm or back. Most important was to let our patient know that we cared.

The clinic approached our potential patient, Robert, to see if he would consider having a support group. At first he rejected the idea, but then he realized that his mother would soon need support.

It was the middle of December when another member of the class and I had our first meeting with Robert, his mother, one of the clinic staff members, and our associate pastor. Robert explained that he was doing this for his mother. Her name was Doris and we liked her immediately. She lived in a small town about 30 miles away. Robert chose to live close to the hospital where he received his treatments.

Robert had been an executive with a large organization in another state. He worked as long as he was able. Even after moving, he held a part-time job for a while. When we became involved, Robert was no longer able to work, but he had a car and was still able to drive. His health was pretty good at this stage and this gave us time to become acquainted. He soon decided to become involved with our Bible study group. One Sunday morning he arrived early, picked up the class roll, and mentioned that he didn't see his name. Robert became the only single adult member of our Young Married Adult Bible Study!

Soon things started to change. When doctors told him he could no longer drive, he really started regressing. Although a federally funded program provided some necessary services such as bathing and changing linens, he depended on us for food, laundry, and help with appointments. He still wanted to be a part of the class activities, so class members brought him to Bible study and class socials. Many of us would take him out to eat to provide a change of scenery.

One hot day near the end of July I was to take Robert's lunch to him. I called to see what he was in the mood for, and he said he was really craving chili! My heart sank. I didn't want to make a pot of chili in July! I asked if canned would be all right, and he said he preferred the chili at Wendy's. I discovered that Wendy's didn't make chili in the summer, but Krystal did. I became a big Krystal fan after that.

When I finally arrived at his apartment, he was sitting on the sofa. He didn't get up, which was unusual, but asked me to put lunch in the kitchen and he would eat it later. I sat down with him and we talked for a long time. When it was time for me to leave, I asked if I could pray. I didn't always do this, but that day it seemed like the thing to do. I remember taking his hand and holding it during my prayer. I don't remember exactly what I prayed, but I do remember thanking God for Robert and for his friendship. That was the last time I saw him. He died the first week of August.

Robert was right. His mother did need us. When we minister to one person, the ripple effect often includes family and others. Our pastor and associate pastor went to see the family, and many of us attended the funeral. A young lady from our church choir sang a song that Robert had selected. We helped Doris clean out Robert's apartment and made several trips to different organizations with items for donation. For several years I've sent her a note in April around Robert's birthday.

I have learned that everyone, no matter what condition he or she is in, needs love and friendship. People who are the hardest to love need love the most. That is why Jesus was found among them so often.

❧ Decisions, Decisions

In Wyoming where I lived for many years, if you encountered a person having car trouble out on the road, you stopped and gave assistance. Leaving someone stranded in the cold of the Wyoming mountains or plains could be lethal. On a number of occasions, I stopped to assist people in trouble and provided a ride into town as needed. As a result, I am comfortable with evaluating a situation and stopping to give assistance.

After moving to Alabama, I was on my way to work when I saw a woman and her child walking in the median of a very busy highway. I had passed their broken-down car not long before I saw them. It was obvious they were walking to get help. No one was helping them, even though they were in a dangerous place between rushing traffic. I stopped.

When I offered my assistance, the woman refused to get in my car. I assured her that my car was safer than where she and her child were walking. Even then, she hesitated to trust a stranger with the life of her child and herself, but she finally gave in and allowed me to take her to safety. I still laugh when I think how hard I worked to convince her to let me give them a lift.

Helping a woman and child on a busy highway is a no-brainer, as one of my friends would say. A few days later, one of my co-workers told me that the woman I assisted was her neighbor. Her husband had recently accepted a position at a local Christian university. The woman told my friend how much she appreciated the assistance although at first she was concerned about getting in the car with a strange woman. She was amazed that someone would stop to help.

Small experiences that seem insignificant at the time equip us to make decisions on down the road. How many people passed the woman and her child that day and did not stop? What kept them from seeing her need? Fear? Busyness? Lack of experience with persons in need? I was amazed at how far this woman had walked by the time I came by. Multitudes of people could have assisted her before I arrived on the scene. Yet I was the first to help. No doubt my experience in Wyoming prepared me to make the right decision that day.

❧ Other Teachers

Some time ago I starting writing notes in my Bible. I have recorded significant comments about passages and marked important verses. I have recorded dates of important spiritual events, names of people for whom I am praying, or what I have heard God say to me. I have also recorded prayers or commitments I have made to God. Since I read through the Psalms several times each year, I have marked each psalm with a date so I will know immediately which psalm to read on any given day of the year.

Today I was looking for a particular verse in the Book of Psalms when I came across the prayers I recorded for my father after discovering that he had untreatable cancer. The day we were told the terrible news, I wrote these words by Psalm 90: "8/30/99 Today we learned that Daddy has untreatable cancer. Bangor, Maine, Dr. Fry." I had also written a note by Psalm 90:10. "Please, Lord, 80 years, healthy, painless, for my father." My father was 72, and I claimed this verse about long life for him. The next day I read Psalm 91. I underlined verse ten and wrote beside it: "Heal my Father, Lord!" In the next psalm, I underlined verse 14, which reads "In old age they still produce fruit; they are always green and full of sap." Written beside Psalm 93 is "You are greater than the floods or disease."

I am reminded of my desperation at the time and of my confidence that God could heal my father or at least help us to find the experimental treatment that would extend his life and decrease the pain. Surely if we prayed enough, God would hear and answer our cries. Isn't that the way it works?

My father's illness was untimely. Yes, he was spiritually prepared, but he did not want to die. He was full of life. He and my mother were enjoying the finest years of their life serving in their church, traveling, playing golf, and visiting with friends and family. They were in good physical condition, careful about their diet, and exercised on a regular basis. Anyone who met them was impressed with their energy and enjoyment of life. For these reasons, I felt that there must be a way to overcome this horrible disease.

My father died in November. He did not see his next birthday. Am I to conclude from this experience that God doesn't heal or that God doesn't answer prayer?

A woman in our community, highly respected by her church and family, was accused of a serious crime. Regardless of the testimonies of her supporters and the evidence that she had been used by her employer to cover up his own illegal activity, she is serving time in prison. Everyone except the judge believes she is innocent. Her church, friends, and family have been in concerted prayer for her deliverance. Are we to assume that God cannot save us from the injustices of our world?

Experience isn't the only teacher. Experience alone cannot confirm for us the reality of who God is. Our experiences must be measured against Scripture and against the broader context of God's work through the ages. God looks upon our situation with the eyes of one who can see all that has gone before and all that will follow. He knows perfectly what is happening within the human body and all that is thought and felt by the human mind and heart. Meanwhile, we are looking at and responding to only what we can see with our temporal eyes and hear with our temporal ears, and feel with our temporal hearts.

In *God Came Near,* Max Lucado reminds us of the two followers of Jesus who met Him on the road to Emmaus after

Jesus' death and resurrection. Their words were filled with lost hope. "But we were hoping that it was He who was going to redeem Israel" (Luke 24:21 NASB). Lucado goes on to say that the two on the way to Emmaus were limited by "their lack of vision. Their petitions were limited to what they could imagine— an earthly kingdom."

God's promise to us is that He is always working for good toward those who love Him. When I look at my experience with God, I realize that He is faithful to His word and that, even in the worst of situations, He loves my family more than I can comprehend. Perhaps this thought alone is the most significant for me as I put experience in the right context. For you see, I think I love and care for family, friends, and the world; but in comparison to God's love and care, mine is pale and weak, often selfish and shortsighted.

Thinking back on my father's situation, I would have done anything to make him well or to take away his pain. At the same time, I realize without a shadow of hesitancy that God knew better than I knew what my father needed most. God would not withhold one good thing from my father for He loved my father perfectly.

Do you recall Job's response to the loss of his children, his wealth, his health, his status, and his friends?

"For I know that my Redeemer lives, and that at the last he will stand upon the earth; and after my skin has been thus destroyed, then in my flesh I shall see God, whom I shall see on my side, and my eyes shall behold, and not another." (Job 19:25–27)

Job knew that his experience was not the whole picture of God's love and concern for him. He knew that God had not abandoned him and that God was faithful in all situations. Perhaps the book of Job is provided so that you and I can see that our experiences are only part of the story of God at work in our lives.

As for my father, I have often thought of the title of C. S. Lewis' book, *A Severe Mercy*, for we experienced God's mercy in that my father's suffering was shortened. It did seem severe, for our loss was great. But the wonderful loving Father did what He knew was best when those of us with limited vision could not comprehend the scope of God's love for us all.

Your personal experiences tell the story of God's gracious goodness. Writing this book has been an intimate experience for me since many memories have resurfaced. Some have come back like sharks' teeth and others have been gentle breezes filled with song and laughter. All of them have been moments of reflecting on how God is evident in all the times of my life.

Take time to reflect on the experiences that prepared you for today. Praise God for using your life events—great and small—to help you live an extraordinary life.

Chapter Seven

Surrounded by Giftedness

I see Christ
In your life,
I learn about Christ
Through your life,
And now I want Christ
In my life.

Reuben Welch wrote one of the most inspiring books I have ever read. His words come back to me often, and I find myself reading once again his call to community. The name of the book, *We Really Do Need Each Other*, is also the topic of the book. God has called us to community, but we still tend to live in isolation. We undervalue what we can offer one another and how much we need each other.

Years ago I attended a large training event in New Mexico for church leaders. One workshop included both new leaders and experienced leaders. The workshop leader divided the conferees into small groups. She included a mix of experienced and inexperienced leaders in each group and gave each group several assignments through which the experienced leaders would mentor the new leaders.

As a new leader, I was in awe of the ideas and knowledge of the others. Their illustrations, testimonies, successes, and failures were more than my mind could take home. The wealth of help and encouragement I received in just two hours made all the difference for me when I returned home.

We really do need each other! The Lord has surrounded us with people we need and people who need us. Many of these are people filled with the Spirit of God, using their gifts, skills, and talents to touch the lives around them and throughout the world. Let me introduce you to a few that I have met. Hear their stories of God's extraordinary work in ordinary people. You will discover that these women have experienced many of the same joys and sorrows that are common to life, but still God is at work doing what only He can do. I think you will see that God's work is endlessly diverse in each and every life and that the ways in which He touches the ordinary to make it extraordinary are indeed delights we can each experience.

✌ A Celebration of Family Gifts

When looking at gifted people, the best place to begin is with your own family. Often we fail to see the wondrous giftedness in their lives. We take for granted their skills. We may even fail to voice appreciation for who they are. We may go through a lifetime with unspoken affirmation of the value of our family. In the preface of *Woman to Woman: Preparing Yourself to Mentor*, Edna writes that "today's mobile Baby Boomers are the first generation of Americans who live far from extended family—those who provided in-house mentoring experiences for the previous generation of women. Though not able to define the void in their lives concisely, today's women often flounder in life experiences without the support and encouragement of more mature women who have traveled the road and weathered the storms successfully."

Perhaps my story of family will encourage you to take a closer look at those with whom you share a heritage. You may even decide to be hostess to the first family reunion your family has ever had. My excitement grew as I walked off the plane in Dallas, Texas, to meet my mother and my granddaughter who were flying in from Colorado. We were going to the ninth reunion of my mother's family, the Holloways. My nine-year-old granddaughter Chelsea was about to meet the Texas part of her heritage and had brought dolls and other important items to share with the new cousins she was going to meet.

When we arrived at the lodge, we joined more than fifty other people linked to the name Holloway by birth or marriage. From the oldest of nearly eighty to the youngest of only a few months, family members came because they wanted to share more than just a name. They wanted to practice being family.

I knew that this was no ordinary family when my aunt mentioned the family business meeting, an important part of the yearly tradition. All the adults gathered to hear minutes from last year's meeting and a brief financial report. My aunt said a few words of memorial for family who had died during the year, including my father. (Although he had married into this family, he was a committed family reunion participant.)

Awards were given to several people for being either the oldest, the youngest, coming the farthest, or for being there for the first time. The wooden awards were handmade by my cousin Charlie and his wife Cheryle. Charlie worked throughout the world, and he and his family learned to appreciate many different cultures. Even so, it was clear they are holding on tight to their Texas roots. After all, once a Texan always a Texan!

Reunion events included an auction to raise money for the family cemetery, a bingo game, and even a fireworks display. But the highlight for me was visiting with my cousins and aunts. I discovered that I am blessed with a family who cares and gives their best. For instance, my cousin Randy and his wife Debra use their medical expertise as doctor and nurse to bring healing to the people of Honduras where they go each year with medical teams. Randy's brother, Rhad, has taken up flying, and his wife Kathryn works in ways that allow her to be available for their daughter, Belle. Lori, Lisa, and Bryant are full of banter and charisma. When we played bingo, Bryant's calling had me in hysterics with laughter. I discovered that both Lori and Lisa are actively involved in organizations that deal with issues affecting women, children, and families in significant ways. Since their father couldn't be at the reunion, their mother Paula willingly shared a room with all the little girls (most of whom left their beds during the night to crawl into beds with their mothers or grandmothers).

Bryant's daughter Austin and my granddaughter Chelsea developed a sweet friendship. Chelsea shared her dolls, and Austin taught Chelsea to dive into the pool. When Bryant's wife Sherea told me she is a manicurist and gives luxury two-hour pedicures, I wished that I had made an appointment with her. Carolyn Lee, Darlene, and Glenda are sisters who "gift" their aunts, uncles, and cousins each year. This year they brought handmade calendars with original art by Carolyn's husband, Merl. They are also working on the family genealogy. Who knows what discovery they might make about us some day!

My cousin Bill and his wife Dinah cooked Texas barbecue for the big family meal on Saturday. When he isn't cooking at the reunion, he is a welder who does heavy equipment repair. His young son, Lance, was very proud of a photo of him standing inside the shovel of one of the largest bulldozers I've ever seen. Russell and Marilyn are cousins who grew up around horses, raise horses, and passed that interest on to their children. Their families have numerous awards to show for their involvement. One of my youngest cousins, Angela, is a gifted pianist and physical therapist. I discovered that she and her husband Sam love cats and met in a singles department in their church.

The talents and skills of my cousins came primarily from my aunts and uncles. Aunt Mozelle is surely the prayer warrior in our family and a faithful letter writer to those of us who are away. Aunt Frances is delightfully fun and assured me I would enjoy sharing a bedroom with her and my mother. She was right. Aunt Jane brought my favorite food, watermelon, Texas style of course. When I heard that my Aunt Lois would not be at the reunion because of the illness of my cousin Steve, I knew that I could reach out to them through my prayers. Families who take time to not only laugh together, but to pray together and for one another, are the strongest and most blessed families of all.

Uncle Max led in cooking breakfast the first morning we were there. Max, like so many in my family, is a man of many talents. He farms, gardens, ranches, does both construction and interior design, and the list goes on. On the night of the fireworks, his wife Carolyn and I shared a few words about the common loss of her parents and my father. That meant a lot to me.

Families provide a wealth of knowledge about who we are and how we can live, about the choices we can make, and about the ways in which we can use our skills. I know that from the short time that I was with my extended family, I have been challenged by the ways they chose to use their time and talents.

I discovered that love of God and commitment to His mission run deep in these of whom I am one. Our shared faith is the only bond that will join us together for eternity. Being around them and others not mentioned was an encouraging spiritual exercise, one I recommend to anyone with extended family.

A Few Gifted Women

You and I are surrounded by gifted people. The following stories are those of a few of the women who have crossed my path. Their stories celebrate the unique work of God in each life. These women are representative of many whose stories I do not have room to tell. I have chosen women from a variety of backgrounds and situations so that you might see how God is living among us wherever we are and whatever we might be doing, giving extraordinary lives to ordinary people.

Sandi Rives, Homemaker, Alabama

Sandi Rives is a member of my church. I admire Sandi and have seen in her life a deep commitment to God's purposes. She chose to be at home to raise her children and to continue her work of ministry through her church and in the community.

Growing up, Sandi was involved in Bible schools and mission activities. Today she continues to find ways to reach out to others. Sandi and her husband Jim recently redecorated their home so it would be even more accommodating to ministering to people and hosting large groups.

In our church, she teaches young couples and sings in the choir. Through the couples class she is involved in ministry and evangelism and enjoys helping visitors to the church find their place of belonging. Sandi made a significant decision years ago that she would not work so she could remain home to raise her children, practice her gift of hospitality, and be available to volunteer through her church.

While many women do not know what their spiritual gifts are, Sandi has discovered that along with the gift of hospitality, she also has the gifts of ministry and mercy. She has been involved in an outreach to people with AIDS and a service called Stephen Ministry. Through this ministry she has been trained to provide Christ's healing love on a one-to-one basis to people experiencing anything from illness and grief to family troubles or a job loss.

Her training included the art of listening, sensing others' feelings, compassionate assertiveness, maintaining confidentiality, praying with people, and finding help in the Bible. She also learned to recognize needs that require professional help and how to refer an individual to appropriate counselors, physicians, or community agencies. Her training in this ministry continues twice monthly so that she can become more and more effective in walking with persons through crisis.

Sandi has discovered that the gifts and skills she uses in her "spiritual" life are needed in the "secular" world just as much. She has been asked to read Scripture in one of her civic groups and was asked to serve as secretary for her golf group (which includes sending notes of sympathy). When on jury duty, one of her fellow jurors asked if there was a preacher in the group who could prayer for the jurors before they began deliberations. Sandi wasn't a preacher by trade, but she was able to pray for all twelve jurors and provide God's touch as the jurors deliberated a criminal case. Sandi's life affirms a statement that she made to me recently: "Someday I will cease being amazed at how many opportunities God provides for me to use these gifts in everyday life in touching others for him."

Sarah Standerfer Groves, Musician and Author, Arkansas

I knew Sarah as a co-worker and friend. When she left our city and moved with her husband to a new place of ministry, she had just finished writing *A Seeking Heart,* which reveals her heart for God. She writes, "In one way or another, we all have a seeking heart. Our hearts yearn for God's touch, even when we don't realize it. Our lives get dry and need to be filled with God's wellspring of love. We become more like Christ and more aligned to God's desires for our lives. Our seeking hearts find their homes in God and we are made whole, changed by His presence in our lives." (from *A Seeking Heart* by Alicia Williamson and Sarah Groves).

Sarah began her worship of God as a young girl. At the early age of 13 she already knew she wanted to serve God through ministry and worship. She can remember the first woman she saw leading music at a youth camp, and knowing that she wanted to do exactly the same thing when she grew up.

God does have a plan, and Sarah's desire to lead in worship was in line with her natural talents as a musician. In fact, Sarah admits that her life has always revolved not only around God, but also her love for music. Through piano and voice lessons she graduated to playing solos, playing and singing in a rock band, and serving in various ways through her church music ministry.

Godly women who used their gifts as speakers and worship leaders continued to influence Sarah's life. She remembers "hearing women speakers when I was a youth and in college encouraging those present to 'do our best today, so we will be ready for the doors that God opens.' " The words of admonition strengthened Sarah to remain steadfast toward the purpose that she felt God had for her.

Another significant influence for Sarah was her parents. Sarah's parents have been involved in church and denominational ministry throughout her life, and have provided support throughout Sarah's ministry experience. To this date she has served as a public school music teacher, camp director and music/worship coordinator, youth minister, and youth consultant for a national Christian mission organization. She leads seminars, speaks for women's events, and leads worship at retreats and conferences. And for several years now she has been the wife of Mark, who is a church minister of music.

Sarah recently gave birth to a beautiful daughter, Gracie. The joy of this time is heightened for Sarah and Mark since Sarah experienced a miscarriage a few years ago. Their grief was deep, but I watched them allow God to touch their lives with healing.

Although Sarah has known loss and disappointment she has continued to remain steady toward her purpose. She wrote to me these words: "I determined a life vision statement when I was in college and I have kept that same vision as a guide in my choices and decisions to this day: 'My purpose is to love God, love others, and be the best I can be with the gifts God has given me.' God has been faithful to open up doors of opportunity and ministry . . . faithfully and consistently. I believe he is honoring His calling on my life and my commitment to follow."

God does honor faithfulness by opening new doors of ministry for His children. Sarah has a growing ministry as a composer and has had a book of her music published. God has taken a "private" part of Sarah's life and is now using it to bless others. Sarah described God's leading: "For several years I have been writing music, more for my personal worship than for sharing with others. The songs have been intended primarily for the intimate time I have with God. Even so, now the doors are opening for me to put some of these songs into the hands of others as a published music author and this has led to a fulfilling new ministry."

Karry Wainright, Administrative Assistant, Arizona

I have known Karry since she was a teenager. I had the joy of seeing her come to Christ and then mature in Him. When I sang at her wedding a few years ago, she actually identified me to her friends as one of her mentors. Considering the depth of her Christian commitment, I am honored to be numbered with those who have shaped her life.

When Karry went to seminary, she had no intention of becoming an administrative assistant, but through this ministry she has been able to participate in aspects of ministry that she had never considered a possibility. She enjoys the "behind-the-scenes" tasks, such as keeping the office and files organized, and preparing what is needed for various meetings that her supervisors are involved in each day. Since some of her work has been on church staffs, her work has often included other ministries of the church.

Karry discovered quickly that she is the first contact many have with her office, which gives her a unique opportunity to provide a positive image. She is able to provide help and give the information a customer may need. To do this she has intentionally learned what resources, materials, and assistance are available through her office.

Since Karry is a perfectionist, she is the one in the office who insures that every letter and publication is free of typos and grammatical errors. She understands that for many persons the written communication they receive may be their only impression of the persons that Karry works with.

I have watched Karry wait on God. Her plan for her life was different, but her faith has held her true to His plan. She waited for the perfect man, and now she is married to Mark. She wanted to work in an area that was more pioneer to the gospel, and now she is living in area where the need for Christ-followers is great. Karry has not allowed the questions and lifestyles of her friends to turn her from God's plan for her. I can hardly wait to see what He will do with her next!

Debra Bell, Government Administrator, California

Debra radiates both concern for others and an inclusive spirit. She is a natural mentor, with women in her Christian circle looking to her for wisdom and leadership. And she's never been afraid to express her faith as a civilian administrator on a military base. Along with her abilities to organize and manage people, she has received numerous promotions. Even when she decided to retire, her supervisors offered her more promotions to encourage her to stay just a while longer.

Debra says, "Working in a government office in California has provided many opportunities to use my skills. I know that those under my leadership as well as my peers are looking at the way I live in the workplace. As a Christian and a supervisor, I was restricted from discussing politics and religion with my employees. I often had to find ways to express God's love in other ways rather than conversation about God."

The respect and trust her employees have in her is evident in the response of one of her staff members. Debra is a popular Christian seminar speaker, and is also involved in planning seminars for women. When one of her employees discovered she needed help with her handouts, he volunteered his time after work to do some of the handouts on his home computer. The result was that he became interested in the content on the handouts and began to ask about them. Eventually, Debra told him about a ministry in which she needed some one to teach computer skills, and he volunteered his services as a teacher. Now he is teaching two days a week, arrives early to participate in a Bible study class, and is asking questions and showing an increasing interest in Christ.

Debra shows the same kind of love and respect for her family that she shows to co-workers. But it's not always easy. "My son worked as an art producer with rock bands and concert artists, where he often encountered and worked with persons who were into drugs and alcohol. At one point, a nightclub owner insisted that my son include topless dancers in his work. My son had the moral courage to reject the demand and to explain that it was against his religion and that he had been raised to respect women and their bodies.

"I was concerned about his career choice, and for years I tried to convince him that he needed to get out of that environment. While I knew that he had to make his own choices, I still continued to pray that he would get another job in a different environment. Finally he reminded me that I had raised him to know Christ and that he could reach more people in one night for Christ than I could in a month."

Not long ago Debra asked her daughter what she thought of how God had been evident in their relationship. Her daughter expressed her joy in their special mother-daughter relationship where she feels confident in sharing her needs with her mother, knowing that she can trust her mother to pray.

Debra has grown throughout her Christian experience. She remembers one time of renewal while worshiping in Germany. "I was listening to a woman sing 'How Great Thou Art' in a worship service when the sun came over the mountains to fill the windows of the sanctuary with light. A dove was sitting on the windowsill and I felt a renewing of my spirit. I rededicated and committed my life completely to my Father. The true re-fining of my skills is tested as I reach out and touch others. I am encouraged when I see greater willingness to serve God, for then I know that God is strengthening and blessing me."

Jean Langenbach, Registered Nurse, Pennsylvania

Jean and I have never met; but when I looked for a nurse who exemplified Christ through her life and work, several people recommended Jean's name.

Jean's walk with God began when she was seven years old. She had been ill for a year with numerous throat infections that made it necessary to have her tonsils removed. That meant an overnight stay in a hospital and her first time away from her parents' safety and protection. She saw other children crying and bleeding in her ward and feared that she would also be in their situation. After her surgery a young woman in a white dress was standing beside her. She was so impressed as a little girl by the caring spirit of this nurse that she knew from then on that she would someday be a nurse.

Jean not only felt the call to nursing, but later in her child-hood she felt God's call to missionary service. After completing nursing school and working for several years, she married, and her plans for missionary service were put on hold. She raised four children and went through a painful divorce. As never before she found that she had to lean on God's strength to see her through.

When her children were grown, Jean re-entered the work world as a hospital nurse and discovered that God was not through with her. She tells her story in this way: "I spoke to a client who was concerned about her sick, elderly sister. I suggested that she bring her into the clinic. When she did, the doctor and I discovered that the woman was very sick indeed. She was dehydrated, running a high fever, and had an open bedsore. We had her placed in the intensive care unit, but she passed away two days later.

"Through this one woman, my eyes and heart were suddenly opened to the needs of the elderly, many of whom were falling through the cracks in the health care system. Medicare was not meeting all of the medical needs of our elderly. Many needed financial help as well as assistance in their homes. I strongly felt that God wanted me out of the hospital setting and into the homes of the frail and elderly.

"It was not an easy switch, but God was by my side as I made the move which required additional training. Administrators, pastors, doctors, community social service workers, and many others helped to guide me in establishing a Christian health ministry in the Northeast. We sought donations for our ministry. Through God's grace and direction, funds were found that have enabled us to provide subsidies for our patients in need. We have been able to provide skilled nursing care, in-home services, home health aides and homemaker/companions, and training for all of our workers. Best of all, we also provide help for the spiritual needs of our clients."

Jean thought for a while that her dream and call of fulfilling God's purpose for her life were dashed, but God once again showed that His grace and sovereignty are greater than our human frailties.

Alice Newman, Pastor's Wife, Hawaii

Alice is one of those women whose graciousness and giftedness is evident from the moment you meet her. She is truly beautiful inside and out and a natural mentor to the women in her life. I have seen the evidence of her Christian beauty in the strength of her ministry with women who are following in her footsteps to become great leaders in calling women to God's mission.

Alice became active in church during her teenage years, and knew quite early in life that God was calling her to be a pastor's wife. She married Ken and has now been a pastor's wife for more than 45 years. Her role has included teaching an adult women's Bible study class and serving in the mission ministry of her church. She became a paid staff worker with her state denominational office with the responsibility of women's ministries and missions. Her love for children led her to start the childcare center in her church where she worked as director/teacher, and saw the ministry grow to include over 200 children daily.

As if all this wasn't enough, Alice has the gift of hospitality. I've stayed in her home, and know many other people who have had that blessing, and we all agree that she is the absolute perfect hostess. Her meals are works of art, her home is decorated to perfection, and yet she makes you feel as though you are the reason that her home exists. Living in Hawaii has given Alice plenty of opportunity to practice this gift since so many people love to visit the "Aloha" state.

Alice recently retired and is envisioning opening a bed and breakfast in her home. She is already making plans for how that might work so that she and Ken can host tourists, missionaries, and their many Christian friends from around the world.

When I say from around the world, that is exactly what I mean, for Alice is also deeply committed to a ministry with international students. She and Ken now have about 30 'adopted' adult children from Mainland China. Five have come to know Christ and Alice wants to become more active in this ministry in the years ahead.

Alice believes that she and Ken have had a shared ministry, which includes four sons and six grandchildren. As she begins her retirement years, she writes, "I know that God gives us love for the people with whom He calls us to serve. Although my husband and I are not native to Hawaii, we have been here for more than 39 years. This is our home and we plan to continue to serve God in this place. Our hearts are with the island people, a love that God has nurtured through our years of ministry."

Carmela Bartels, Missionary

Carmela was a featured missionary speaker at one of the annual board meetings of the organization where I serve. I will never forget her testimony of the tragic loss of her child that led her to discover God's faithfulness. She openly shared her struggle, and I heard many comments about her honesty and her courage.

She found strength in God's word. "One passage that I often share is 2 Corinthians 1:3–4: 'Blessed be the God and Father of our Lord Jesus Christ, the Father of mercies and God of all comfort, who comforts us in all our tribulation, that we may be able to comfort those who are in any trouble, with the comfort with which we ourselves are comforted by God.' (NKJ) The two names of God that are given in this verse are a great beginning for meditation. *The Father of Mercies* assures us that He will have mercy on us. *God of all comfort* affirms His comfort of us. We are also assured that there is purpose to our suffering—we will be able to comfort others and point them to our merciful Heavenly Father who will also comfort them. These verses remind me that all suffering has a redemptive purpose. I try to share these verses with others as the Lord gives me opportunities to do so."

Carmela knows what it means to lose hope in the future and turns to Jeremiah 29:11 for God's promise of welfare. She loves to share this verse with others and tell them about her own renewed hope as a result of this scriptural promise. "The promise was so personal. I grabbed that verse and claimed it for my life. In time, I began to see God fulfill His promise as He provided a new job in a new place, and He gave me another child. His name is Jeremie, which means *the Lord will be exalted.* Psalm 107:21 (KJV) says, 'Let the redeemed of the Lord say so.' That is what the Lord has convinced me that I must do. He has given me the gift of faith and I must say so."

Carmela knows that God has called her to encourage others through the sharing of Scripture and the ideas that He communicates through His Word. She is thrilled in sharing her faith with others because God's encouragement is real and relevant to the here and now.

As with all Christians, Carmela is on a journey, which has now led her to a new awareness that she is to be involved in one-on-one evangelism. At first she was afraid but excited about having the honor and privilege to lead someone to the Lord. So she prayed, "OK, Lord, I am willing to do this and prepare myself, but You will have to bring the people to me. I do not plan to go door-to-door witnessing. I am not ready for that."

God did bring persons to Carmela. The first experience came when she visited a home during follow-up visitation after Backyard Bible Club. Not long afterward, she had a flat tire and a young man assisted her. With joy Carmela affirms, "As a result of these two opportunities, a kindergarten teacher and a young gypsy man came to know Jesus Christ as Lord."

Lenora Pate, Attorney-At-Law, Alabama

Although Lenora has been recognized as one of the ten most influential women and one of the top five most influential lawyers in Birmingham, and is a member of my church, I didn't meet her until she was running for governor of our state. Her outstanding qualities are evident in her ability to run a household, negotiate contracts, teach an adult Bible study class, run for governor, speak throughout the state for tax reform, mental health, women's issues, healthcare reform, and other concerns, and all at the same time. Lenora has also had a significant role in the defeat of gambling in Alabama in recent years.

Lenora sees a definite link between faith, truth, her success, and her profession, and knows that God gives her wisdom liberally as she makes decisions that have profound effects on the people involved. While her clients, partners, and opponents may not be aware of her source of wisdom, she knows that God often "drops His wisdom in my spirit, with strong urgings or leanings" and she knows that He is the one who enables her to think on her feet when in the middle of serious negotiations. Lenora may be unique from some attorneys in that she prays for people on both sides of the issue.

Lenora knows from experience the pain that life conflicts can bring. When her children were small she encountered the heartbreak of divorce. At that time she had been a stay-at-home mom, and now faced raising two sons alone. She was devastated. Now as she looks back she can see how God used this experience to make her more like Christ as she entered into a relationship with God that she had not had before.

After her divorce Lenora decided to go to law school for what she confesses may have been both right and wrong reasons. Even so, God was leading and protecting her, and has used her in mighty ways for His purposes. Her work as a attorney opened doors for her to serve as the first woman director of the State of Alabama Department of Industrial Relationships, and she now has influence through numerous Christian and secular boards, commissions, and organizations with which she serves. She is a shareholder with a major law firm in the Birmingham area. Lenora has discovered that every time a door closes, God opens another.

God's faithfulness has encouraged Lenora to become a "Bible junkie." She often rises early to study the Bible. She also has learned to use the time she is drying her hair, driving her car, or doing other activities as quiet time to meditate on Scripture.

Lenora knows that she is continuing to discover all that God has planned for her life and is not afraid to walk with Him into the future. She hasn't decided whether to make another run for governor, but is open to whatever God has for her around the next corner.

❧ *Mentored by Gifted People*

Women such as these mentioned above are mentoring other women as they live out their relationship with Christ. Women are watching and learning from their lives. For a few years, I volunteered at a shelter for homeless women. One night as I was leaving, one of the women followed me outside. She asked me if I would mentor her and help her get back on her feet. What a delight to chat with her on the phone, see her at the shelter, and then to take her and her daughters to church with me. After a while, she was coming to church on her own and was bringing other women from the shelter with her. She was soon able to return to her hometown and continue reestablishing her life. Several years later, she was working at one of the malls here in town and helped a woman who happened to be a member of my church. When she found out that the woman knew me, she sent me greetings and a positive word about her life.

All of us need mentors, people to encourage us and to walk us along the journey of life. Author and speaker Esther Burroughs explains that we need mentors because we have a need to be nurtured; we need support as we find ourselves in new places; we need communication that is from the heart; we need acceptance; and we need relationship.

Not only do we *need* mentors, we *are* mentors. According to Tricia Scribner, a mentor serves, encourages, teaches, counsels, and guides. You and I find ourselves in these roles often, either intentionally or unintentionally, for we never know who might be watching us.

I was in Chicago's O'Hare airport with a long layover and decided to have a Chicago-style hot dog. If you've ever had one, you know that it is heaped with every imaginable vegetable, pickle, and sauce—an absolute masterpiece of a hot dog. I paid a large sum for the hot dog, and as I turned to walk away, the hot dog jumped out of my hand, did two flips, and landed upside down on the floor in front of a very large audience. The hot dog gave a fine performance. The only thing missing was the applause. Needless to say, I was embarrassed and would have preferred to walk away and pretend the hot dog was not mine. I tried to play it cool and gathered a handful of napkins and cleaned the remains from the floor. I started to leave when a woman spoke to me. "Aren't you Andrea Mullins?" she said. I realized this woman had been watching me the whole time. I recalled everything I had said or done in the last thirty minutes. I was so glad I had cleaned up that hot dog with a good attitude for this woman had been in many of my conferences.

While it is true that Jesus is the only perfect model for how we should live, it is also true that Jesus reveals Himself through the lives of those who love Him. When you are looking for a hero, look around at those who love God. Don't look for perfect people. Look for those who know that they need God and have found Him through His Son, Jesus Christ. Look for those who humble themselves before others but are secure in knowing that God has a plan for their lives and has lavished them with His good gifts. Look for those who understand that they have been blessed so that they might in turn bless others. Look for those who know that they have an extraordinary God who gives ordinary people extraordinary lives.

Chapter Eight

Divine Direction

Sitting by my Father's side, the road map on my lap,
I saw the pathway loom ahead.
The crooked road, the narrow way,
"The way's too steep!" I said.
But in the pathways of my mind, I saw the years behind,
His faithful reading of the road, His leading ever kind.
And so the tears from all my fears
No longer trailed my cheeks.
And the path that rose to greet me,
Was the very road I seek.

Reading road maps was nearly a cultural trait in my family. Traveling from state to state was a requirement for my father's career in the oil industry. Sometimes I would ride beside him in his welding rig and read the road map for him while my mother and sister followed us in the family car. As with all families, traveling made for some humorous situations. I recall one trip that took us through Cincinnati. My father was pulling our small mobile home with his truck, and my mother was driving the car. Somehow we got separated from my father as we drove along an urban interstate during heavy traffic. We were keeping an eye out for my father when we looked across several lanes of traffic to see my father on another interstate going in the opposite direction.

Fortunately, such experiences were rare and by the time I reached adulthood, I felt like I was an extraordinary map-reader. I knew I could find my way to any place at any time. This was my attitude when I invited a well-known speaker and trainer to assist me with a conference. She was to go with me to visit churches around Wyoming where I lived and served. The speaker's name was Evelyn, and I assured her that although I had not been to the city of Powell, I knew how to read a map and we would reach our destination as planned.

A few hours into our trip, a road crew that was dynamiting the canyon walls to widen the passageway stopped us. Sitting there enjoying the beautiful scenery and the nice weather, I asked the woman flagging traffic how much further to Powell. When I asked the question, the woman nearly broke out in hysterical laughter as she explained that we had traveled for over an hour in the wrong direction. Evelyn laughs still as she tells the story of the long trip we made after we turned around. We arrived at the church in Powell almost an hour and a half late, and the congregation was still there waiting on us.

Road maps do not give us all the information we need for a journey. If you look closely, you soon discover that most places have numerous routes for arriving and departing, not counting the options of going by car, bus, train, and plane. Do you want to take the shortest route or the scenic route? Do you want to be behind the wheel or let someone else handle the traffic? Are you in a rush or do you have lots of time to kill? We have many decisions when choosing the direction we want to take.

Before you become totally confused, let me put your heart and mind at ease. Unlike a road map you read to get from town to town, the road map for your life has a perfect compass. You do not have to search out the paths of your life. God has the road map, and He knows every route to every place in your journey. Reflect on these assurances from God, captured in Scripture long ago but written with you in mind.

"O Lord, you have searched me and known me. You know when I sit down and when I rise up; you discern my thoughts from far away. You search out my path and my lying down, and are acquainted with all my ways." (Psalm 139:1–3)

"Though the Lord may give you the bread of adversity and the water of affliction, yet your Teacher will not hide himself any more, but your eyes shall see your Teacher. And when you turn to the right or when you turn to the left, your ears shall hear a word behind you, saying, 'This is the way; walk in it'." (Isa. 30:20–21)

"You show me the path of life. In your presence there is fullness of joy; in your right hand are pleasures forevermore." (Psalm 16:11)

From the time that God began to establish His people, He made clear that He knows the way and He alone is responsible for guiding us in the way. The Lord gave Adam complete instructions regarding what he was to do in the Garden of Eden. The Lord counseled Cain so he would know what kind of offering was acceptable. The Lord guided Noah to the perfect vehicle to insure his family's future. The Lord told Abram the route to take and what to do along the way. The Bible offers a story, transcending centuries and generations, of God giving His people directions. No one must remain without future, hope, or purpose. God does have a purpose for your life and He will give you the directions for arriving at the right place at the right time.

I am convinced that we sometimes fear knowing God's purpose for our lives and His planned directions for getting there. I've heard many testimonies of missionaries who as children or teenagers were afraid to respond to God's direction for fear He would send them to Africa or China or some other undesired destination. Some of the stories of the Bible seem to reinforce this dread, such as Jonah being sent to Nineveh, Daniel in the lion's den, or Jeremiah in the well. The list goes on. The reality of these stories and all stories where God is in the lead giving the directions is that the ending is always a true success and leads to God Himself.

❧ *Following a Divine Road Map*

A few years ago, I began to write out what I sensed God purposed for my life and some of the goals that might guide me toward that purpose. I did not realize how important this practice was until my father's seventieth birthday. My mother was giving him a party, and I decided to fly to Texas for it. Since the party was on Saturday evening, I would stay over through Sunday. My father asked me to sing in their church for the morning worship service. When he called and asked, I was busy and did not feel I had time to find the right song or to practice. When I told him I could not plan to sing on this visit, I could hear the disappointment in his voice. After hanging up, I remembered two of my life goals. One is to use the talents and gifts God has given me at every opportunity that comes my way, and the other is to be a blessing to my family. How could I not use the talent God had given me to bless my father on his birthday? I called him back and said I rethought the situation and I would sing. When the time came, I had a song to sing, and God's blessing and presence were evident.

Since I can be easily sidetracked from the direction for my life, I have found that having a written statement reminds me of what is most important. I want to stay focused on God's direction for that is when I live with passion, and the "a-ha" of life is a frequent reality. Most people want to know who they are and the singular purpose for their lives. For the Christian, the desire to please God deepens our quest for the answers to these questions. Not only do we long to know God's direction, but He longs to provide it because He is a loving Father.

❧ *Guided by a Loving Father*

The search for divine direction begins in knowing that God is a loving Father. God, the Creator of the universe, has come to you as a loving parent. He made you His child. Ephesians 1:5 tells us "He destined us for adoption as his children through Jesus Christ, according to the good pleasure of his will." You are blessed to call God "Father." Paul used this intimate title in Ephesians 1:2, as he sent grace and peace to the Ephesians from "God our Father and the Lord Jesus Christ." Ephesians 1 affirms for us the pleasure God experiences in making us His children. Having a loving Father provides security in seeking God's divine direction since our status with Him is based upon His unconditional love and acceptance. God did not choose you because of your beauty, money, education, popularity, or success. Your place in God's family does not depend on your ability to balance your budget, use a computer, or bake a cake. God chose you because He loves you. What better way to show you His love than to make you His child, and who better to trust for divine direction!

❧ *Pleasant Boundaries*

God the Father does love you. As with any loving parent, He set boundaries that bring the greatest fulfillment. God's boundaries for you are pleasant boundaries. The psalmist sang, "You have enclosed me behind and before, And laid Your hand upon me" (Psalm 139:5 NASB). The Psalmist knew that God determined the framework in which His life would reside and that God was with him guiding him along the way.

Think about your boundaries or the framework within which you live. When someone asks you to describe yourself, how do you respond? Do you say "I'm single" or "I'm married with children" or do you regale them with tales about your grandchildren? Maybe you describe your job, give your professional title, or relate your educational background. Do these describe some of the pleasant boundaries through which God is giving your life direction? These descriptors we use to define ourselves are those boundaries within which we find our accountability. Here are the places where we discover the passion for living that forms the basis of our purpose.

God has given each of us pleasant boundaries. The boundaries may change through the years as He guides us, but His desire is that we enjoy fulfilling daily relationships and meaningful work whether we are corporate executives, college students, mothers of young children, factory workers, or great-grandmothers. If our boundaries are different from someone else's, fine. God's direction is available to all of us; we have equal access to passion-filled living.

How does this happen? How can the boundaries of being at home with six small children be as fulfilling as the boundaries of a beautiful, sought-after speaker? The wonderful reality is that all boundaries are pleasant when seen as places where we will find our guiding passion. Then our most mundane tasks will take on a new meaning.

Consider the value of any relationships when we begin to understand the impact we can have on those around us. Imagine the urgency of planning how we use our time when we realize that the time we invest in God's pre-planned good works will have supernatural influence. After all, can't a divine encounter with the grocery checker change a life as quickly as the pastor's sermon on Sunday?

❧ Signed, Sealed, and Delivered by the Holy Spirit

Boundaries are not all that God has provided to give our lives direction. He has also provided the Holy Spirit. The Holy Spirit enters our lives, a reminder that God will not quit guiding us until we have reached our destination. In other words, when God begins writing His purpose on the pages of our lives through the Holy Spirit, He writes on our lives with permanent ink. Or as Eugene Peterson states it in *The Message*, we are "signed, sealed, and delivered by the Holy Spirit" (Eph. 1:13).

Not only does the Holy Spirit remind you of God's continuing guidance, but He also inscribes in your life all the wonderful promises of God. Think of your life as a book, with beautifully illustrated pages. When you look closely, you see that every page is inscribed with these promises: *Blessed, Chosen, Loved, Forgiven, Called*. Sometimes you may see worn edges or loose binding, but don't be discouraged if the corners are bent. The most beloved books always have worn edges and loose binding. God's good words are still there. Sometimes you may think you have to squint to see His promises, especially when you are busy or tired. If you look carefully, you will see that God is still there. The Holy Spirit reminds you again and again that God fulfills all His good promises in your life.

Consider for a moment what this means for you. It means that God's promises go with you through every circumstance.

Take a few minutes to leaf through the pages of your life book. Look for God's promises that are imprinted on every page and take time to meditate on each one.

Begin with the promise of being *blessed*. "It is for this that you were called—that you might inherit a blessing" (1 Peter 3:9). The greatest blessing of all is the presence of God, and with His presence come untold other blessings through which He validates His direction for you. How is He blessing you? What do you learn about God's direction for your life?

Look for the promise that comes from being *chosen*. "You did not choose me but I chose you. And I appointed you to go and bear fruit, fruit that will last, so that the Father will give you whatever you ask him in my name" (John 15:16). Because you are chosen, God cares for you as a parent. His greatest joy is to give you the desires of your heart. He wants your life to bear fruit, to be abundant and fulfilling. Listen for His voice reaching out to you as His child. What are your desires? What good things do you see happening as you serve God? How do they speak to you about God's direction for you?

Look for the promise of being *loved*. "I pray that you may have the power to comprehend, with all the saints, what is the breadth and length and height and depth, and to know the love of Christ that surpasses knowledge, so that you may be filled with all the fullness of God" (Eph. 3:18–19). God's love for you does not depend on any action of yours. His love is unconditional. The breadth of His love will embrace you wherever you go. The length of His love spans time, from before you were born through all of eternity. The height of His love means He will see you through to completion and will bring you to your eternal home with Him. The depth of His love means you cannot fall low enough to be beyond His forgiving love. What evidences of His love have you seen along the road, and what do you learn of His divine direction?

Look through the pages of your life for the promise of being *forgiven.* "If we confess our sins, he who is faithful and just will forgive us our sins and cleanse us from all unrighteousness (1 John 1:9). Jesus Christ has freed you to fully embrace the direction of God's leading. Is there anything you want to confess to God now that may be keeping you from following Him? Accepting God's forgiveness releases us from unnecessary guilt. Is your vision for the road ahead clearer when sin and guilt are removed from the way?

Look for one more wonderful promise, simply the promise of being *called.* "I therefore, the prisoner in the Lord, beg you to lead a life worthy of the calling to which you have been called" (Eph. 4:1). God calls you to serve, using the gifts poured into your life through the Holy Spirit. God calls you to share the love of Jesus. God calls you to pray for those who are hurting, for those who are without Christ. God calls you to give of your time, of your resources, and of your skills. Divine direction will always lead you toward your calling, which is to go with God to a lost and hurting world.

Divine direction is for right now. Think for a moment about today. What is the priority for this day? Remember God's promises for today—*blessed, chosen, loved, forgiven,* and *called.* As we think about setting goals for our lives and understanding our purpose for living, we have a divine reminder that we can live according to God's divine direction.

ເ♠ *Purposeful Living*

Many contemporary books provide guidance for defining your purpose, writing purpose statements, and setting goals. You may want to buy a book that gives more detailed information, but perhaps I can help you get started thinking about and writing a purpose statement for your life as well as setting goals toward that purpose. Find time to draw aside with God to let Him reveal

His wondrous love and direction for you. The ideas that follow may help you to begin the journey to extraordinary living.

Organizing Your Life
God's divine direction may be hidden amid the clutter of your life, but you can begin to see the light by taking some simple and important steps. Try these simple steps and see if your life could use a little organization.

__ Remove clutter.
__ Group items that go together.
__ Eliminate items that do not belong.
__ Contain items to keep them from becoming cluttered again.
__ Assign items a place and a priority.

Richard Foster, a Quaker writer, challenges us to simplify our lives in his book *Freedom of Simplicity*. He encourages us to discover the contentment that comes when we put our lives in order. He gives specific ways to accomplish this. One way is to spend more time in silence, allowing God to speak to our inward desires. Another is to maintain a healthy cycle of sleeping, eating, working, and playing. A third way is to understand our limits, which means we refuse to live in a chaotic frenzy of activity. Order is perhaps the beginning of disciplining our lives and can provide a freeing experience for following God's direction.

ᦰ *Discipline as a Lifestyle Habit*

Following God's direction will likely call you to a greater sense of discipline. Three important areas of discipline in every life are money, sex, and power. Foster discusses these disciplines in his book, *The Challenge of the Disciplined Life*. The three broader contexts are business (money), marriage (sex), and government (power). Foster writes, "Business refers to the task of bringing forth the goods and services of the earth either to bless or oppress humankind. Marriage refers to the human relationship par excellence that creates the context for either the deepest possible intimacy or the greatest possible alienation. Government refers to the enterprise of human organization that can lead toward either liberty or tyranny."

God's direction is concerned with these disciplines of life. Looking at the boundaries and promises of God that are uniquely yours, consider how each of these disciplines would be applied in your life:

Business: What are the goods or services that God would have you make or give that will bless mankind? This refers to talents and skills and how you choose to use them.

Marriage: What would God have you do in relationship to your family that will allow for the deepest possible intimacy? On an even broader scale, this refers to relationships that you have with family, friends, and others.

Government: What social issues does God want you to help change that are holding people in bondage? Hunger, poverty, abuse, illiteracy, and medical needs are just a few of the areas of need where you could make a difference through your prayers, your ministries, and your citizenship responsibilities.

Can you write a life purpose statement with a goal for each of these areas? Defining God's desire for these three areas of your life could change your decisions regarding the future.

🍃 *The Balancing Act*

Most of us have heard that life should be prioritized in a certain linear order such as

God
Family
Church
Work
Witness
Self

I struggle with this prioritizing method and feel that the approach of J. Grant Howard is more biblically sound. In his book *Balancing Life's Demands*, he says the question is "How do we put God first?" Does this mean that we give our families less time or that we read our Bible while we are supposed to be working? He suggests that rather than putting God first, we put Him at the center of all we do. Howard directs our attention to Matthew 22:34–40. Two commandments are given. Jesus refers to loving God as the first commandment and loving our neighbor as the second commandment. Jesus also makes it clear that we are to love ourselves for that is the way we are to love our neighbor. Howard explains that the *first* and *second* are not ranks of the two commandments but only a listing, such as *1* and *2*. Jesus said that the second commandment is like the first. When #2 is fulfilled, then #1 is also fulfilled. Howard writes: "We have learned a simple but profound truth. Our basic responsibility is twofold—love God and love our neighbors." The point is that the two are equal in importance and one cannot exist without the other. Howard states that we have three responsibilities in life: God, our neighbor, and ourselves. Scripture does not rank these for they are inseparable.

Can you define a life goal for each of these three responsibilities? I have provided a sample goal for each.

- *Love of God*: I will spend an hour each day with God in study of Scripture, meditation, and prayer.

- *Love of neighbor*: I will say and do toward family, friends, coworkers, and others only those things that will enable them to know and accept God's love.

- *Love of self*: I will use and develop my talents, skills, and gifts with every opportunity God provides.

❧ *Measuring Our Success*

An airline magazine that I often see profiles CEOs that are considered to be models of success. When I read these articles, I usually learn something about what makes a person successful. The articles discuss their values, their business practices, and characteristics that others have recognized in their leadership styles and that have contributed to their success.

According to Sheila West in *Beyond Chaos*, success can be measured in various ways. She mentions three ways that I think have relevance in determining our purpose for living.

- *External success*: What is it that I am doing with my life that is making a difference in the world?

- *Internal success*: What values do I live by that reveal integrity of character?

- *Eternal success*: How am I enlarging God's kingdom?

Our ultimate purpose is extending God's kingdom, but breaking down how we are using our talents, resources, and time into the three categories listed above is helpful.

Sheila's book offers assistance to the working woman who is looking for order as she tries to balance home, work, and all the issues that cause stress in both worlds. She lists six ways in which Jesus modeled focus toward purpose.

1. Jesus understood that His agenda was to preach about God.
2. Jesus clearly knew His purpose was to save the world.
3. Jesus knew that His power came from God alone.
4. Jesus' only aim was to please God.
5. Jesus did only those things that would enable people to have abundant life.
6. Jesus never strayed from His purpose, even to the point of death.

When you examine these characteristics of Jesus, you find that His life reflected external, internal, and eternal commitments. How does your purpose for living compare to His? Jesus knew what true success was all about. He was the perfect model of humanity and the only One through whom we can truly understand godly success.

Marilyn Henry, associate executive director at a major Birmingham hospital, would certainly be a success in anyone's book. While God's direction has been foremost in her life for many years, she never dreamed she would one day be in the position that she now has. In fact, she would not have considered it a possibility. She did not even know it existed. In fact, it did not exist before it was offered to her. It was a new position.

Marilyn knows that living in obedience to God has opened doors for her. Even if she had designed a twenty-year plan, her plan would never have been as extraordinary as God's plan. Her approach has been to put God first and hone her skills as a nurse and as an administrator. At each crossroads, God has been faithful to show her the way to take. She has learned to trust in His divine direction. If you measured Marilyn's life commitments against those of Jesus listed above, no doubt you would find that Marilyn's faith in Christ has led her to live according to His model.

❧ Writing Your Mission Statement

Christ has shown us how to live. Christ has shown us who God is. Christ has shown us why we exist and who we are. So where is your passion? What is it that is uniquely you in this wonderful journey of God's direction?

Sometimes putting our thoughts in writing confirms God's leading and gives us guideposts for staying the course. Do not be afraid to write it down, for a written statement can be changed as often as needed to keep it relevant to your life. Are you ready to give it a try?

Kimberly Douglas of Douglas Consulting provides some definitions that may help you to think through what you would like to write. I am including some samples to clarify what I believe each of these represents.

Mission statements (I call these my purposes for living) define the road on which you are traveling: *I am accountable to God to serve all people with selfless love for the sake of the gospel of Jesus Christ.*

Value statements (I call these goals) define the guardrails along the road:
• *I will find ways to enrich Mike's life daily.* (value my marriage)
• *I will bless my family through actions and words.* (value my family)
• *I will use my gifts and talents at every opportunity.* (value my spiritual gifts and talents)
• *I will tell others about Jesus.* (value my relationship to Christ)

- *I will be honest and dependable in my life and work.* (value integrity)
- *I will nurture my current friendships and make new friends.* (value my friends)
- *I will be actively involved in global missions.* (value God's mission)

Vision statements (I call these objectives) define the mountain that you are traveling toward or your destination: *My aim is to please God in all I do and am.*

❧ *Setting Goals to Hold You on Course*

How do goals help you to stay on course? Each value statement I have mentioned is broad in expressing what I value, such as blessing family, using gifts and skills, and sharing Christ. Under each of these value statements, I add action steps. Let me use one of the value statements to illustrate how this works.

I will bless my family through actions and words.
- I will pray concertedly for Mike, Michele and family, Mama, Kathy, Rachel, and Mike's parents.
- I will pray for other family regularly.
- I will visit, call, send cards and gifts, and email to family.
- I will stay in touch with aunts, uncles, and cousins.
- I will express love verbally give forgiveness, and ask forgiveness.
- I will meet needs that I discover—financial, emotional, spiritual.

Notice that the action statements tell how I will live out my value system. You may not want to write down every action statement (I don't write them all down, either), but such lists provide a measurement for how well you are living out your goal.

Get a cup of tea, a cola, or a cappuccino, your favorite pencil, or go to your computer, and begin writing. Who knows all that you will discover about your extraordinary God who is working in you to give you an extraordinary life.

Look for the Extraordinary Work of God

Turning the corner
I was caught off guard
And my heart was touched
By the lives that were marred
With the sin of the ages
And the pain of the years
That told me I had seen
Where Jesus was slain
And still He was there
In the midst of it all
And waiting for me
To answer His call.

Chapter Nine

In Your Life

A small lump of clay
In the Potter's strong hand,
A turn of the wheel,
Shows the life He has planned.

Now the word of the Lord came to me saying, 'Before I formed you in the womb I knew you, and before you were born I consecrated you; I appointed you a prophet to the nations.' Then I said, 'Ah, Lord God! Truly I do not know how to speak, for I am only a boy.' But the Lord said to me, 'Do not say, "I am only a boy"; for you shall go to all to whom I send you, and you shall speak whatever I command you. Do not be afraid of them, for I am with you to deliver you, says the Lord.' " (Jer. 1:4–8)

The words of the Lord to Jeremiah are as relevant to us as they were to Jeremiah in his time. God was working in our lives before we were born. He has a plan and He never sleeps or rests from giving us whatever is needed to see His plan accomplished.

From time to time when I am concerned for a family member or a friend, and they are separated from me where I cannot see what goes on daily, I begin to think that my prayers are of no effect in their lives. *God, are you really able to work this out?* I begin to question. I never cease to marvel when I become aware of what God has been doing, and I am always humbled.

In the same way, God continues to be present and active in our lives. He does not try to hide His existence from us. Instead, He wants us to be alert to see what He is doing in us and through us. He wants us to be able to follow Him and go with Him every moment of every day. The Lord went on to say to Jeremiah, "You have seen well, for I am watching over my word to perform it" (Jer. 1:12). In other words, "I am working continually to bring to pass all that I said I would do." God affirmed Jeremiah for seeing the things that God was showing him.

Simply stated, God is at work in your life. How can you recognize where He is working? As you read the rest of this chapter, you may begin to see where God is at work for the first time. The direction you are taking may be affirmed, or perhaps you will be more alert to the many ways that God is at work so that you can continue in the extraordinary life He has given you.

❧ *Open Doors*

When my friend and coworker Carolyn Weatherford Crumpler experienced an open door of opportunity some years ago, the possibility was so pleasing to her that she was afraid to walk through it. She wondered if her own desires were blinding her to God's true intention for her life. She hesitated to step into this new role of service. After struggling with the decision for several days, she decided to speak with her pastor, a friend whom she felt she could trust to be forthright with his counsel. She explained her dilemma. How could she know that God was opening this door? How could she tell the difference between her own desires and God's will?

The pastor listened to her concerns and responded thoughtfully. The answer came in looking at the decisions and choices she had made throughout her lifetime. She had determined long ago to follow God's lead and to participate in His purposes. God's will had been foremost in her life activities. She had always seen her life path in relationship to God's concern for a lost and hurting world. Now she was offered a position through which she could lead Woman's Missionary Union, a Christian women's organization, in calling churches to God's mission.

The pastor explained that as we follow Christ our desires are replaced by His desires. A lifetime of obedience results in the mind and heart of Christ. What pleases Christ also pleases us. We want what Christ wants. The open doors that please Christ also please us.

The discussion ended with the question, "Is it possible that God will be as delighted as you when you walk through this open door?"

The Lord knows the distress that often is experienced as we seek to follow Him. No one knows better than He how much we want to see the handwriting on the wall telling us exactly what to do. God knows that our human desires can be powerful distractions when confronted with an open door that looks appealing.

In a recent conversation with a young man in a significant position with a national non-profit foundation, I heard his story of open doors. He had been in a financially rewarding corporate position that brought little personal fulfillment. When the door opened to work with the foundation, he willingly left a high-paying position to provide the non-profit organization with his expertise. He knew that this was what he wanted, and he had served there for five years.

Now he is struggling with the next open door. He has a family, a baby on the way, and numerous open doors to financially rewarding positions across the nation. He is facing a dilemma of too many open doors, many of which are tempting. He has enjoyed his work at the foundation, but it offers no advancement. What should he do now? I remember times when my husband could scarcely find a job, and then within days more than one job offer would come in. What confusion that brings.

What do we do when we stand in front of an open door? Or several open doors? Believe it or not, God has a plan for such a time as this.

"Out of my distress I called on the Lord; the Lord answered me and set me in a broad place." (Psalm 118:5)

The psalmist cried out to God in the midst of his distress, and God answered him. Not only did God answer, but the gateway also became broad and protected. The psalmist realized that he had God on his side and that he could take refuge in the Lord.

The broad place is for anyone who is distressed, regardless of the cause of the distress. All God asks is that we call on Him for direction and wisdom. Psalm 118 goes on to say in verse 27, "The Lord is God, and he has given us light." God does not leave us in the dark, wondering whether this is the gate for us. He wants to lighten our eyes and heart so that we might recognize the doors He has opened.

If you feel that the door might be the right door and you have not received the word *no* from the Lord, then take a step toward the door. In speaking with a prospective employee recently, she said, "I have not received a clear *yes*, nor have I heard a *no*, so I feel that I should continue with this process." Since we both still felt the door was possibly the right door, we made an appointment for her to come for interviews. She had taken the first step, trusting God to show her whether this door is right for her.

Doors will open that are not the right way for us to go, but through a prayerful attitude we can discern the difference if we ask questions and allow God to answer us.

• How do you hear God's voice and see God's presence in this?
• How does the open door agree with your life purpose?
• How will the open door enhance the ministries that God has gifted you to do?
• How will the open door add value to family responsibilities?
• Will anyone else be hurt if you go through this door?
• What will be the cost?
• What will be the gain?
• How will this open door contribute to the Kingdom of God?

Make your list of pros and cons. Then let God show you how they measure up. When my husband and I had a long list of reasons not to go through a door that had opened, we took it to God. Within days God had turned every negative into a positive. God works in amazing ways to affirm for us His chosen doors.

Remember that God is a God of affirmation. He will affirm our right decisions, and He will always answer the cries of the righteous to deliver them from distress. So the psalmist went on to sing:

"Open to me the gates of righteousness, that I may enter through them and give thanks to the Lord. This is the gate of the Lord; the righteous shall enter through it. I thank you that you have answered me and have become my salvation. This is the Lord's doing; it is marvelous in our eyes." (Psalm 118:19–21,23)

Yes, our God is Lord of the open door. He comes into us at our bidding and shows us the blessings that come with following Him.

≈ Closed Doors

My volunteer team had traveled many miles to reach the former Soviet Union. Our goal was to distribute Russian New Testaments. Most women in the group had received financial assistance from their churches to be able to participate. After all, this was one of the first groups to go into Soviet states with free reign to take and distribute Bibles to the people. Everyone's excitement and anticipation were riding high. Our mission was covered on the local television and radio stations. We were interviewed before hundreds of listeners, and many prayed for us and longed to be a part of this incredible experience.

We knew that many persons and churches invested their time and money in our team. We arrived in Moscow and successfully completed our assignment of sharing Christ wherever we could and giving Bibles to as many as possible. Our next stop was to be Frunze, Kirghizia. We had shipped Bibles from the United States to Frunze so they would be waiting for us when we arrived. When we arrived, we discovered that the Bibles were not there. They had not arrived. We were devastated. What were we going to do? What about the investment so many had made in our lives to allow us to be there?

One young woman on my team was especially distressed. She felt overwhelmingly responsible for the financial commitment her church had made in her trip. Team members comforted her as she wept over the situation, frustrated that the very purpose for which we had come seemed to be hopelessly blocked by a situation out of our control.

The only option left was to trust God with our time and obligations. We gathered in my hotel room to discuss the bad news. We prayed and asked for God's hand upon our lives. I asked each woman in the room to name the gifts and skills she had that God might use in this place. One by one the women told how they could make a contribution. Again we prayed and asked

God to open new doors now that this one had closed.

The next day we met with the church in Frunze. The Christians here had lived through the worst of persecutions. They were few, but they were powerful. They worked hard and seldom had time for fun and fellowship. For years, they had lived in this Muslim state under the heavy hand of Communism. Now for the first time, for a short time, they had freedom to worship openly. We heard the stories of how they used weddings and funerals as worship sessions. Then we were blessed to participate in the wedding of two of their young adults. They asked us to sing, to bring greetings, and to speak. We hugged and kissed and hugged and kissed some more. We saw a baptism. Perhaps the most striking memory was the overflow of people who gathered at the church to worship on both Saturday and Sunday. The church was full to capacity with people waiting on the outside to come in.

We were humbled when we heard the prayers of the elderly women. Although we could not understand the words, our hearts responded to their passion as they lifted their voices to God in praise and worship. These were the women who had prayed for the walls of communism to fall. These were the women who lost husbands and sons for the cause of the gospel. We could teach them methods for Bible study and developing ministry, but we had much to learn from them about praying and commitment.

Before our visit was over, every woman in my group had used her abilities and gifts in some way. We saw the power of God work through us to encourage and equip these newly freed Christians to be ambassadors for Christ in the city of Frunze. We had developed new friends on the other side of the earth, a place that I feel most certainly is *the ends of the earth* of Acts 1:8.

Doors do close in ways we often do not understand or appreciate. When the apostle Paul was on his way to Asia, the Holy Spirit forbade him to continue in that direction. The Scripture says that "they attempted to go into Bithynia, but the Spirit of

Jesus did not allow them" (Acts 16:7). Paul was fortunate in his frustration. That very same night, God revealed why the door was closed. "During the night Paul had a vision: there stood a man of Macedonia pleading with him and saying, 'Come over to Macedonia and help us.' " (Acts 16:9)

Most of the time when doors close before us, we do not see an open door as clearly and as quickly as Paul did that night. Many of my friends have experienced closed doors to needed jobs and closed doors to places where they wanted to live. Missionaries have had to leave the countries and people they loved because of political unrest or unapproved visas. Numerous couples struggle with miscarriages and the unful-filled desires to have babies. Some couples have had numerous delays in adoption processes.

What does a closed door mean to ordinary people who have an extraordinary God?

God knows exactly what we are facing. He knew it before it occurred. "Your eyes beheld my unformed substance. In your book were written all the days that were formed for me, when none of them as yet existed" (Psalm 139:16).

God cries with us. "We do not have a high priest who is unable to sympathize with our weaknesses, but we have one who in every respect has been tested as we are, yet without sin" (Heb. 4:15).

God comes to us as helper in our times of disappointment and discouragement. "And I will ask the Father, and He will give you another Helper, that He may be with you forever" (John 14:16 NASB).

God can be trusted with the situations of our lives. "You show me the path of life. In your presence there is fullness of joy; in your right hand are pleasures forevermore" (Psalm 16:11).

God will give us strength to live with and through the closed door. "Those who wait for the Lord shall renew their strength, they shall mount up with wings like eagles, they shall run and not be weary, they shall walk and not faint" (Isa. 40:31).

God will give us peace in facing the closed door. "Indeed it was for my own peace That I had great bitterness; But You have lovingly delivered my soul from the pit of corruption, For You have cast all my sins behind Your back" (Isa. 38:17 NKJV).

God will open the right doors at the right time. "I have seen the business that God has given to everyone to be busy with. He has made everything suitable for its time; moreover he has put a sense of past and future into their minds" (Eccl. 3:10–11).

The doors we had hoped for may never open in our lifetime, but we are to live for today, seeing what God has for us right where we are. God's instructions to the Hebrew people in bondage in Babylon are still true for us today.

"Thus says the Lord of hosts, the God of Israel, to all the exiles whom I have sent into exile from Jerusalem to Babylon: Build houses and live in them; plant gardens and eat what they produce. Take wives and have sons and daughters; take wives for your sons, and give your daughters in marriage, that they may bear sons and daughters; multiply there, and do not decrease. But seek the welfare of the city where I have sent you into exile, and pray to the Lord on its behalf, for in its welfare you will find your welfare." (Jer. 29:4–7)

The Lord intends that we live the extraordinary life He has planned for us. Closed doors are as much to guide us toward that life as open doors. Our closed doors are open doors to God's continual blessings. Once again we discover God's sufficiency for extraordinary living.

🐦 Good Job

One week at my daughter's home gave me the opportunity to see my grandson Patrick play softball and my granddaughter Chelsea play soccer. That week was Patrick's last game. The team had not had a great year, but Patrick's commitment to winning was not lagging a bit. He stepped up to home plate, focused his eyes on the ball, and hit with all the power that an eight-year-old has. As soon as the ball left his bat, he sprinted to first base. He easily moved around the bases, stealing bases and running when others made hits. His confidence and skill paid off when he completed a run for one of three team points.

The next day was Chelsea's first soccer practice day. She put her heart into doing her best. When she announced that she was trying out for goalie, we knew she could do it because she did not have to be pushed to work hard. Sure enough, the next week she was named goalie for the Tweetie Birds fourth-grade soccer team. In just one week, she had practiced until she could kick the ball well over half the length of the field.

Meanwhile at both games, Mommy, Daddy, Grandmommy (me), and all the other relatives present were yelling, "Good job!" Needless to say, we were very proud of Patrick and Chelsea.

Not every child that plays in sports is a great athlete. Not every child that plays the piano will become an accomplished musician. Not every child that writes a story will become a good writer. But Patrick and Chelsea have shown growing natural skills in athleticism, which allow them both to excel in sports-related activities. They have heard "good job!" often, not only because their families want to encourage them, but also because they are good at what they do.

We all want to hear the Lord say to us, "Well done, good and trustworthy slave; you have been trustworthy in a few things, I will put you in charge of many things; enter into the joy of your master" (Matt. 25:21). The potential for hearing this is great for each of us because God gives us what we need to do the work we are called to do. The Holy Spirit continually teaches us and shows us what it is that God has given us to enable us to do His work.

You are already hearing these wonderful words, "Good job!" from the Lord. His "good job" may not be in audible words but is heard in the peace of mind that comes from obedience, and the sense of "feeling His pleasure" when we use the gifts and skills that He has given us.

God wants you to do a good job with your life, and He affirms you in many ways. You are not dependent on hearing what others think of your service, although it never hurts to hear a word of encouragement and appreciation from our fellow believers. I have listed things in life that may be ways we hear the Lord's admonition of "good job!" Are any of these things happening in your life? If so, then perhaps God is saying to you, "good job!"

- You have been offered a new larger responsibility.
- The group you are leading is growing in size and commitment.
- People in your life are coming to Christ.
- People in your life are growing in their hunger for more of Christ.
- You have a growing awareness of God's presence and leadership.
- You are having more opportunities to share Christ or touch lives using your gifts and talents.
- You have a growing hunger and commitment of time to be with God in prayer and Bible study.
- You have an irresistible urge to share Christ.
- You love being with other believers.
- You have a sense of "feeling His pleasure."

❧ Change Points

I am convinced that before a change in direction for my life there is also a physical change that takes place around me. Work seems different; people seem different; situations seem different; life seems different. The world seems to be caught in a breeze. My life feels like a tree with the leaves responding to the changing seasons—restless, tossing, and shifting to and fro. The autumn leaves especially come to mind as they respond to the early fall winds, seeking to be set free from the limb where they have been comfortably situated all year long. Now, right before our eyes, they begin to change colors, and eventually, claim their freedom and drift away from the place they have known as "home."

On the other hand, the spring leaves come to mind also. Tiny green bumps begin to appear where only brown plain branches had been. Slowly each bump turns into a tiny leaf, very green and still lacking its final shape. With sun and water, the leaf grows to its potential and finally fulfills its responsibility for the summer season.

Change points are those restless times in our lives when we sense that God is up to something new. We hear a new song taking shape in our hearts and lives. We suspect that something is just around the corner, and we begin to anticipate its arrival. I am speaking of those times when we know God is preparing us for the next part of the journey.

We are not always blindsided by our lives. After all, God is perfectly organized. Rachel Scott, one of the young women killed at Columbine High School in 1999, knew that she would die young. The year she died, she had written in her diary months before her death that this would be her last year to live. Is it possible that she was so close to God that the Holy Spirit revealed God's plan to her months before it became reality?

The Lord said to His people, "I am about to do a new thing;

now it springs forth, do you not perceive it?" (Isa. 43:19). "See, the former things have come to pass, and new things I now declare; before they spring forth, I tell you of them" (Isa. 42:9). As always, God prepares us so we can keep up with Him along the way. I believe God has a transition plan, a plan to prepare and move us into the future.

Some years ago, we were about to make major changes in products and ministries our organization provides to churches. We knew that we needed to prepare churches for these changes. We developed an elaborate plan to let churches know that change was on its way. This was a transition plan. Brochures, articles in magazines, information through conferences, training videos, and many other steps were involved along the way.

The *change point* is perhaps God's attention to our need for transition. The closer we are to Him, the more likely we are to be alert to the Holy Spirit revealing God's plan to us ahead of time. Have you heard of persons going through divorces who say they did not know anything was wrong in their marriage? We may experience more change points than we realize when we are insensitive to the leading of the Holy Spirit.

What about those times that you do sense a change is on the way? My husband and I have discovered over the years that when one opportunity comes, two or three others usually accompany it. We agree with someone's statement that life is just one decision after another.

God's wisdom is needed when the winds of change are in the air. Not only may we have to choose between two or more good options, we may even face tragic changes that can knock us off the path and into the briars. We cannot afford to face any change without God leading the way.

We have nothing to fear from change points when we seek God's wisdom. Whatever the change may be, He will see us through it, always to a better place than where we were before. If change brings loss, He will restore. If change brings a new responsibility, He will enable us to do it. If change brings increased wealth, He will teach us how to use it. If change brings joy, He will rejoice with us.

Change is always for our good when God is in the lead. The next time you feel the breeze of change catch your heart, turn to God and say, "Thank you, Lord. I need Your wisdom for each step of this extraordinary life."

"I will lead the blind by a road they do not know, by paths they have not known I will guide them. I will turn the darkness before them into light, the rough places into level ground. These are the things I will do, and I will not forsake them." (Isa. 42:16)

❧ *Opposition*

Benny Delmar, a missionary in the northern plains of the US, had a car accident on his way to preach at a church. His car rolled over, but he was not critically hurt. He got out of the car and hitched a ride into town, arriving just in time to preach his message. After the worship service, he asked if a church member could give him a ride to his car. Only then did the church learn that he had been in an accident.

Benny Delmar was not about to let opposition stop him from fulfilling his call to share the gospel. He knew that our opponent is not human, but spiritual and comes in many forms—even accidents. Do you recognize any of these oppositions in your life?

- Temptation to sin
- Doubting God's saving power in your life
- Thoughts of hopelessness
- Days when everything seems to go wrong even though you made a commitment or planned a task in obedience to God
- People who reject your faith in God

- Unexpected expenses, repairs, setbacks, illnesses, disappointments, accidents, or losses
- Family members who undermine your value or call
- Feelings of guilt and unworthiness
- Lack of appreciation, even rejection, by those whom you serve

The apostle Paul faced many obstacles. In one letter to the Christians in Corinth, Paul listed the opposition he faced. He had been stoned, beaten with rods, shipwrecked, adrift at sea, and in danger from rivers, bandits, his own people, Gentiles, and false brothers. He faced opposition in both cities and wilderness and went without sleep, warmth, food, and clothing (2 Cor. 11:25–27). In his letter to the Christians at Philippi, he wrote, "For many live as enemies of the cross of Christ; I have often told you of them, and now I tell you even with tears. Their end is destruction; their god is the belly; and their glory is in their shame; their minds are set on earthly things. But our citizenship is in heaven, and it is from there that we are expecting a Savior, the Lord Jesus Christ" (Phil. 3:18–20).

Wherever God wants to do the extraordinary is also where you may experience the greatest opposition. Satan will do his best to keep you from seeing that God is doing something mighty in you. Remember that God's power and sovereignty are sure things and that Satan cannot keep God from completing what He has started in you. Christ-followers have an amazing God who is still God, still sovereign, and still has the same power over Satan and all his worldly plans.

❧ Refiner's Fire

"See, I am sending my messenger to prepare the way before me, and the Lord whom you seek will suddenly come to his temple. The messenger of the covenant in whom you delight—indeed, he is coming, says the Lord of hosts. But who can endure the day of his coming, and who can stand when he appears?

"For he is like a refiner's fire and like fullers' soap; he will sit as a refiner and purifier of silver, and he will purify the descendants of Levi and refine them like gold and silver, until they present offerings to the Lord in righteousness. Then the offering of Judah and Jerusalem will be pleasing to the Lord as in the days of old and as in former years." (Mal. 3:1–4)

Ron Boehme tells of going through "a time of great soul-searching and darkness. Everything I'd based my future on came suddenly crashing down. Months of complete spiritual blackness followed." In his book, *If God Has a Plan for My Life, Why Can't I Find It?*, Ron tells of struggling with depression and thoughts of ending it all. He could not understand what God was doing and where God was in all of his circumstances.

You and I are deeply loved by God, the same kind of love that a father has toward a child. Therefore, God is always at work turning us away from those things that are not good and seeking to focus our hearts on those things that are best. He is at work in us to make us in His image so that one day we will see Jesus and we will be like Him. God's character is such that He will never let us remain in our blinded conditions but will continually provide the experiences that get our attention and reveal our true situations in ways we cannot miss.

The refining fire is where God is at work. He is refining you. If you are becoming more aware of God's view of you and you are not pleased with what you see, is this God's refining fire? Don't despair! This is the very place where God is faithful to bring you to completion. Your sin may seem to be hiding the light and you may feel that you are surrounded by darkness when in reality what you are seeing is your own need for God's touch. You may seem alone, but there is no place where God is not present, no place where God is not sovereign, and no place where God's children are separated from Him or hidden from His sight.

Refining fire always prepares us for the next step in God's plan. God wants us to join Him in what He is doing. Without the refining fire, you and I will not see the awesome adventure He has planned for us. A favorite wisdom saying is Proverbs 27:6, "Well meant are the wounds a friend inflicts, but profuse are the kisses of an enemy." God's refining fire comes from His great and never-failing love for us. We can trust His refining fire for we will come out on the other side. The thief hanging on the cross beside Jesus knew this great truth. The thief's dishonesty led to death on a cross, a punishment brought about by his own behavior. He paid a dear price, but as he went through the refining fire, he turned to God. He said to Jesus, "Remember me when you come into your kingdom" (Luke 23:42).

A thief, caught in the refining fire, now lives in paradise praising God for all eternity.

When you see God at work in you as a refining fire, how should you respond? Boehme learned several lessons that are the purposeful outcomes of God's refining fire in any life.

- *Learn the difference between selfish ambition and personal destiny.* Are you doing what you are doing for what you will get out of it or to please God?
- *Learn to wait.* God works according to His timetable, and He knows exactly when we are ready for the next step in His plan.
- *Learn to love God for who He is.* God has proven His character, His faithfulness, and His sovereignty. Our love for Him is not dependent upon our situations or upon God's acting in the way we think He should.
- *Learn to cry in brokenness before Him.* God is looking for broken hearts for only broken hearts can be molded by His love and forgiveness. Jesus said, "Blessed are those who mourn, for they will be comforted" (Matt. 5:4). A broken heart

is better than any sacrifices we can make.

- *Learn true faith, which is primarily forged through affliction.* Affliction releases us from our comfort zone so God can show us how wonderfully faithful and strong He is and reminds us that He alone can provide all that is needed for us to live abundant lives.

- *Learn to die.* Jesus said, "If any want to become my followers, let them deny themselves" (Luke 9:23). Dietrich Bonhoeffer wrote about Jesus' words:

> Self-denial is never just a series of isolated acts of mortification or asceticism. It is not suicide, for there is an element of self-will even in that. To deny oneself is to be aware only of Christ and no more of self, to see only him who goes before and no more the road which is too hard for us. Only when we have become completely oblivious of self are we ready to bear the cross for his sake. If in the end we know only him, if we have ceased to notice the pain of our own cross, we are indeed looking only to him.

The refining fire is a call to die, to die to all our lusts, willful desires, and selfish motives. The outcome is that we join God in the plan He orchestrates for each life and for all nations, an extraordinary plan for ordinary people.

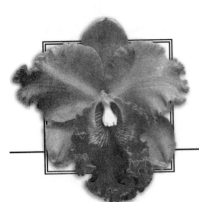

Chapter Ten

In Your Community

You can take a joy ride,
Or a simple walk will do,
To see the other side,
To meet the other "who."
The ones who need your heart,
And those who need your hands,
A place where you can start,
With a simple change of plans.

Mike and I live in Birmingham, Alabama. Our home is here, and our work is here. For the time being, this is our community. We have enjoyed learning about this place and have found our places of service. We both consider ourselves westerners since we were born and spent many of our years in the West. At the same time, we know that this is where we are to make a difference as long as God has us here. We vote, watch the local news, and read the local newspaper. We belong to clubs in the city, and Mike holds an office of responsibility with his organization. We pray for this city, have wonderful friends here, and have been involved in various ministries within the community. We are fans of the Birmingham Barons and Auburn University. We enjoy the banter with friends about local sports and politics. Perhaps most obvious to my western friends is my growing Southern accent!

I have lived in many places, and I know that happiness, beauty, and meaningful service can be found in any community. God wants us to be His ambassadors, His representatives wherever we are, even if we are in prison cells like Paul. God is at work and He has things for us to do that will bless us and bless others. Your community is your place for extraordinary living. Look to see where God is doing His great work and join Him in what He is already doing.

Stay Informed

When Desert Storm broke out, CNN became an overnight success as Americans could not get enough of live news from the battlefield. Minute by minute, the stories and the realities of war came into our homes. Some of us were addicted to the CNN information highway. The result was the development of several ongoing twenty-four-hour-a-day news channels where the latest information can be heard at any time.

Right on the heels of the television stations, the Internet became the *super*highway to the latest news. Now people around the world are in touch with one another at all times of day and night. When I planned a mission trip to Australia, I communicated several times a day with a missionary living there as well as others through whom I was arranging housing and other needs. I can access news or data on almost any subject within a few minutes, drawing from libraries all around the world.

Knowledge is the new bartering tool. Consider the television shows on which participants who know lots of trivia can win a million dollars. The winners are those who have knowledge in many different subject areas. They know what has happened in the past, what is happening right now, as well as what is happening in nearly every area of life, whether politics, government, arts, science, or religion. The few times I have watched one of the popular game shows, I have been amazed at the plethora of information the winners have known.

Even the church is becoming a broker of information. In my denomination, we have videos, more magazines than I can name, numerous newspapers and newsletters, and promotional materials in abundance. The information about worldwide issues and crises is incredible. When a natural disaster strikes any place in the world, I receive emails telling me of plans being made by churches and governments to provide assistance and how I can be involved. The churches in my community have a weekly newspaper that tells needs and opportunities for ministry in the Birmingham area. With so many sources of information available, I have no excuse for not knowing what is happening where I live.

One evening after work, I walked down to the mailbox. A neighbor was out in her yard. I stopped to visit for a few minutes and discovered a whole new side of my community that I did not even know existed. She explained what had been happening within a few hundred feet of my home. I was surprised to hear the stories of guns, threats, and police. I discovered that I was out of touch with my own neighborhood!

Staying informed is an intentional choice you can make. Find out what is going on in your community. Who knows where you will encounter God at work? On the first day that my daughter and I drove into Birmingham, we accidentally got lost in a poor neighborhood. The poverty we saw was shockingly visible. We needed to know that this situation existed in the city where we were going to live. After that, we were accountable for what we learned.

A coworker of mine participated in a leadership opportunity designed to inform influential people about the needs of our city. Over a period of several months, she met other leaders and heard about the issues of our city. Issues included education, government, human services, healthcare, diverse cultures, criminal justice, economic development, quality of life, and other concerns for which leaders are seeking solutions, as well as looking for people who are willing to become involved. From the conversations that she and I had, I know that her eyes were opened to the potential and the need right before her eyes.

The fact that our God has written a book about His work says loud and clear, "I want you to know." "I didn't know" will never stand up in God's court as an acceptable defense. Do you recall the story recorded in Luke 10:29–37? Jesus told of the man who was robbed and left for dead by the side of the road on the way to Jericho. Two men passed by, looked, and pretended not to see. They did not want to know. Only the third stopped to see what had happened and, in response, provided the life-saving care the wounded man needed.

The Lord wants to teach us what He is doing. He wants us to stay informed and invites us to go with Him so He can tell us what He is up to. Read these words from Isaiah.

" 'Come, let us go up to the mountain of the Lord, to the house of the God of Jacob; that he may teach us his ways and that we may walk in his paths.' For out of Zion shall go forth instruction, and the word of the Lord from Jerusalem." (Isa. 2:3)

Across many generations, an organization in my church has provided believers the tools to know what is happening around them and to know how God is working in their midst. Staying informed is the first step toward hearing God's call to go. Most of us will never respond to the social and spiritual needs if we do not know what they are.

The Bible story of Jonah tells how God informed Jonah of the need for repentance in Nineveh. The Lord wanted Jonah to go to this wicked city with God's message of judgment. Once Jonah was informed about the need, he became accountable to respond. He tried to run from God instead. Jonah ended up being spit out on the shore by a big fish that had swallowed him. When Jonah finally brought God's message of judgment, the people responded by humbling themselves in confession and repentance, and God forgave them.

The truths of Jonah's story are as powerful and relevant for today as they were in the days in which the story took place. God wants us to know what is happening so that we might walk into the midst of the need with His message of judgment and hope.

Recorded in Genesis 18 is a significant moment of Abram's life. The Lord visited Abram on His way to destroy two cities, Sodom and Gomorrah. He knew great evils were being committed in both of them. Just as the Lord was leaving for Sodom, He informed Abram of His plans. Read the Lord's thoughts from Genesis 18:17–19.

"The Lord said, 'Shall I hide from Abraham what I am about to do, seeing that Abraham shall become a great and mighty nation, and all the nations of the earth shall be blessed in him? No, for I have chosen him, that he may charge his children and his household after him to keep the way of the Lord by doing righteousness and justice; so that the Lord may bring about for Abraham what he has promised him.' "

From the beginning, God's intention was that we would stay informed so that we could be blessed and in return be a blessing to others. Staying informed allows God to work in our lives to bring about the extraordinary life of His promise.

How should you stay informed?

- Read the newspaper.
- Know the government leaders.
- Be aware of community issues that impact the well-being and spiritual condition of the people.
- Know what your church is doing in the community.
- Be a student of Scripture so that you might respond in a timely and godly manner to the situations that come your way.

?◆ *Community Service Organizations*

Frank is actively involved in an organization that provides various services to those in the community that have needs. Several times each year, he involves our Bible study group in the ministries he is doing through his organization. Frank's commitment to Christ enables him to not only meet physical needs but to also bring the love of Christ to those receiving a helping hand. Frank is in the perfect setting to express the love of Christ to those who need to know.

Another friend participates in an organization that brings awareness about AIDS to the city and has participated in several projects through which she was able to share Christ's love. The making of AIDS quilts, walking for AIDS, and going to schools and churches to provide information about AIDS are just a few ways that she has been involved.

For several years, a group of women from my church has been going to a shelter for homeless women sponsored by a service organization. The sponsoring agency recognized them for their commitment to the ministry. The reputation of the women in the group created a tremendous trust level which allows them to do just about anything they chose to do. Therefore, many residents of the shelter have heard the story of Jesus and His salvation.

One of these women, Ruth Todd, also works with Meals on Wheels. Recently my church recognized her for her lifetime of Christian service. Ruth is involved in taking people grocery shopping and to doctor and dental appointments, sitting with those who are ill, preparing meals for the sick, and at times even helping clean homes.

Many who are in the church see no need to interact through community service groups, but these groups are places where we can learn a great deal about the place we live and the needs of the people who live around us. Not only this, but through these groups we meet other Christians, as well as persons who need to know Christ. Believers need to be where the people are, and this is one of those places we can become involved and make a lasting impact.

❧ *Cruise the Neighborhoods*

A ministry I am involved in required more understanding of a specific area of the city. Each team member was asked to spend time cruising the neighborhood to begin to understand the needs. My husband and I spent a day driving around the area. The business district had empty buildings and a limited number of businesses. Homes were old, many in need of a facelift. On the edge of the city were a number of well-known industries. We learned that these companies employed some of the local citizens but were limited because of educational needs and other issues related to poverty. Poverty was a reality, and the need for access to jobs and continuing education was most visible.

The group I was working with determined that we could make a difference in this community. When I drove through the area, I began to see the needs for myself. Not only did I see the needs, but also I began to care for the people who lived there. Some old and established churches were evident on several corners, and I wondered if we could strengthen the ministries they provided. I visualized what the main street, which already had some nice landscaping and old-fashioned street lamps, would look like with every storefront offering a place to work and a needed product. My commitment to the task of the group was strengthened, as was my understanding of the needs of the people.

You do not have to belong to a group to intentionally drive through a part of town where you have not been for a while. You may even turn down a wrong street and see a need that you did not realize existed. You might take a different route to visit a friend. After driving around the downtown area and seeing the many homeless and how they lived, I did not find it hard to become involved in a ministry with homeless women. Seeing the needs of the homeless has been influential in the involvement my husband and I have had in a food ministry with the homeless and in the items that we donate to various homeless shelters throughout the year.

Ride your bike, take a walk, rent a taxi, or drive your car. No matter how you choose to go, go with your heart open and pliable to God's compassionate response.

❧ Visit Community Mission Points

The pastor drove us to a small railroad town several miles from any other community. The town had no church and no evangelistic witness. We walked the streets and saw the people. We drove across a bridge to a piece of property that overlooked the river. We stood there looking across the water at the homes and businesses on the other side.

"This is where we want to build a church. The developers of

the new housing community have offered this site." The hearts of the small group who stood there were filled with longing to join him in this endeavor. The spiritual needs of the people were great. Drugs and prostitution were common in the community and had even touched the lives of the children. Who could forget the family of women, from little girls through a grandmother, involved in prostitution? Who could understand the lack of interest in God that some had encountered when they visited the homes of the townspeople?

The work of bringing Christ to this small railroad community began. Many hours of visitation, backyard Bible clubs, Bible studies, and ministries to the people set the foundation for the new mission church.

The first church was a mobile home sitting on an unpaved lot. When the rains came, so did the mud. Each week, families from the sponsoring church came to the mobile home to have worship and Bible study. The congregation was small, on some weeks only a few children. Since there was only one teacher for the children and one for the adults, all ages of children went into the same class.

"I have a dream," were the words of Dr. Martin Luther King that inspired millions to stand fast for truth, justice, and reconciliation. In the same way, visiting a place where one of God's servants is passionate about what God is doing can stir the flame of God's gifts in our lives. We can get excited about the potential and be reminded that we have something to offer.

Jesus took His disciples up on a hill overlooking the city of Jerusalem. There He showed them how much He longed for the city below to know God. No doubt joining Jesus at His mission point put in them a longing to participate in His work. How many times Jesus must have talked to them about His concern for the salvation of mankind, beginning in Jerusalem.

Your community probably has a place where a missionary or minister is trying to improve lives and redeem souls. She or he needs what you have to offer. Call the city offices and see if you can find the mission points in your neighborhood. You just might be the encouragement they have been waiting for.

࠾ *Volunteer for a Specific Project*

When twenty-five women volunteered to assist missionary Lynn Latham in her ministry along the notorious Orange Blossom Trail in Orlando, Florida, they probably had no idea they could have such a profound effect on the lives of women living as prostitutes and strippers. Even so, with the support and leadership of Lynn, these women entered strip clubs, topless bars, liquor stores, tattoo parlors, and adult video stores to share the love of Jesus Christ. The result was transformation of women's lives from prostitution and addiction to new lives in Christ and vocations ranging from rehabilitation officers to managerial positions.

If you were to speak with the original twenty-five women who volunteered for this project, I dare say you would find them still serving and still involved in changing lives in their community.

Persons of all ages volunteer. My father-in-law went with a team of volunteers to build a church in Honduras when he was over 80 years old. His service was valuable for he was assigned to handle tasks that freed those who were younger to handle the heavy work in the extreme heat and humidity. He and my mother-in-law have volunteered for all the years that I have known them, helping to build and take care of their church camp, helping to start missions, working with the Billy Graham Crusade, cooking for a mission team in Scotland, taking groups to Israel, teaching and caring for a Sunday School class, and the list goes on. When you have lived your life as a volunteer, you discover a lifestyle that you never want to give up.

If you are just beginning to volunteer and you feel you have limited time, consider volunteering for a specific project rather than a long-term ministry. Specific projects provide ways to test your skills and find your niche. It might be the AIDS walk, a Thanksgiving meal for the homeless, or a prayer walk around a school.

You are a potential volunteer. Can you pray? Can you give? Can you minister? Can you share Christ with another individual? You are lavished with God's presence. Wherever you go and whatever you choose to do, you take Him with you. That's the reward, or the paycheck for the volunteer—God's amazing grace, transforming other lives just as it transformed ours.

Chapter Eleven

In Your World

The world of God's love is as close as His heart,
A world we can see, a world torn apart.
From inside His love our vision is clear;
What seemed far away moves ever more near.

F or God so loved the world that he gave his only Son, so that everyone who believes in him may not perish but may have eternal life" (John 3:16). The prooftext for God's love is not hard to find. He proclaimed and underscored His love for the world throughout the Bible. Creation was an act of love. Judgment in the garden of Eden and in the flooding of the land were acts of love. Calling Abraham to bless all nations was an act of love. Sending prophets and judges, redeeming and forgiving His people were acts of love. Preparing His people for the coming of a Savior was an act of love. Sending Christ was an act of love.

❧ God's Heart for the World

God's love resounds throughout Scripture, but it does not end there. The message of the cross still applies to us.

God loves us today. He still reaches out to every individual, offering relationship, forgiveness, abundant life, and hope. Actually, God's love for the world is the topic of this book since you and I are included in this great love feast that is God's doing. Sometimes we forget how grand it is to say, "God, the Creator of the universe, loves you." We who have been in the church most of our lives hear it so often that the significance of these words is dimmed. Yet God's love for the world is unique—different from any other god-figure or hero throughout the span of time. Good men and women have lived, but none have loved each and every individual as God does.

God's love for the world does come down to the individual. "God loves the world" actually means that God loves each of His creations—each person, each bird, each animal, each creature, each plant, and the whole of the environment. His steadfast and unfailing love separates Him 180 degrees from Satan. Satan hates the world and is doing all that he can to destroy the world and every creature that lives here. He has no regard for individuals. His aims are control, power, and pride.

Scripture helps us to understand that we choose to whom we are going to entrust our lives—to God who has declared and proven His faithful love for us or to Satan whose only aim is to give us exactly what is needed to lead us to destruction. We forget that there is no in-between choice. We really think that no choice is a possibility when in reality there is no such thing.

Every person of knowledgeable age and ability makes a choice every day and every hour of every day.

Joshua clarified this for God's chosen people when he said to them, "Now if you are unwilling to serve the Lord, choose this day whom you will serve . . . but as for me and my household, we will serve the Lord" (Josh. 24:15). Joshua went on to explain that the people could only serve God if they put away all other gods.

We're challenged to understand the depth of God's love for the world when we see those we love suffering from illness or sin; as we look at the hunger of starving people around the world; when we see wars that claim so many lives or governments that are oppressive year after year. "Where is God's love in all of this?" we ask.

A missiologist who spoke in my church asked and answered this very question. First, if God's plan is followed in our world, hunger and poverty will not exist. The Lord laid out a plan for every person's needs to be met, but individuals and governments have chosen not to follow His plan. Even those of us who are believers have more of the world's goods than we need, and few of us have adopted a lifestyle that insures others will have what they need.

Second, the missiologist stated that God may allow hunger, poverty, and war to exist to give us the very places where He would have us to go with Him. His love is revealed through His people, and He wants to show the world and us what He can do when we go with Him into the hardest places of life.

❧ Our Heart for the World

God called those who love Him to also love the world. Let's return to the passage in Genesis, chapter 18. In this passage the Lord told Abraham that the city of Sodom was about to be destroyed.

"Shall I hide from Abraham what I am about to do, seeing that Abraham shall become a great nation, and all nations of the earth shall be blessed in him? No, for I have chosen him, that he may charge his children and his household after him to keep the way of the Lord by doing righteousness and justice; so that the Lord may bring about for Abraham what he has promised him." (Gen. 18:17–19)

God's plan has always included His people. The Lord wanted Abraham to join Him in caring for the people in Sodom. Participating with God in His work was the avenue through which He would bless Abraham.

Often our assumption is that God did not begin blessing Abraham until his son Isaac was born. A closer examination of the story, however, reveals that God did not wait until the birth of Isaac to prepare and involve Abraham in His redemptive plan. God blessed Abraham immediately when He revealed His gracious and steadfast love for mankind. God revealed to Abraham that He does answer prayer. Surely Abraham's faith was strengthened from this experience with the Lord. Read what happened after Abraham heard what the Lord was about to do.

"So the men turned from there, and went toward Sodom, while Abraham remained standing before the Lord. Then Abraham came near and said, 'Will you indeed sweep away the righteous with the wicked? Suppose there are fifty righteous within the city; will you then sweep away the place and not forgive it for the fifty righteous who are in it?' " (Gen. 18:22–24)

Abraham interceded for a people he did not know. He drew close to the Lord to plead for the lives of those who might respond to God's love. Abraham responded in exactly the way God intended for His followers to respond. The Lord knew Abraham's loving the world as God loved the world would bless him. God wanted Abraham to be able to tell his children and his children's children the story of how God responded to Abraham's prayer. God wanted Abraham to know that he and the Lord were in this together and that God would do great things in response to the involvement of his children.

What prompted Abraham to remain standing before the Lord? Why did he choose to draw close to God for these unknown people? Abraham did not know what we know today about God's mission for the world. Abraham surely did not understand what we now call *missions* and he had never heard of a *missionary*. Abraham had not heard that we are to pray, to give, to go, and to do in response to the plan that God revealed in Scripture. Abraham did not have the history of God's mission recorded in the Bible. What moved Abraham to plead with God to spare the city for only ten righteous people?

The answer is found in Abraham's love for God. Anyone who loves God loves what God loves, which is the world. From the beginning, this has been the test of discipleship.

Dietrich Bonhoeffer was a German theologian who escaped from Germany during the Nazi regime. He openly disavowed Hitler and the Third Reich of Germany. When he escaped with his life, his friends encouraged him to remain safely in America rather than return and risk his life. But Bonhoeffer knew he must return. As long as the horrors of the Nazi troops continued, Bonhoeffer felt he must be with his countrymen fighting against this evil. He returned to Germany and eventually lost his life in a Nazi concentration camp.

Loving God results in love for the world. God loved the world to the extent that He gave the ultimate—His Son, Jesus Christ. The same kind of love is expected from those who love God. Bonhoeffer was willing to give his ultimate because he loved God. How deep is your love for God? You are the one the Lord is counting on to love the world with Him.

ᴥ *Where to Look for God's Work*

"Help! Help!" The world is crying for help. The cry is being yelled, screamed, and shouted through our newspapers, our televisions, and our computer screens. We hear the cries for help from those in famine and war, from families and young people, from the elderly and the sick, from the poor and oppressed, and from the devastated and the fearful.

One day in a northern town a man walked into a store and robbed the clerk at gunpoint. He ran and the police ran after him. The police followed his trail that ended near a small two-room house. Thinking the robber had gone into the house, the police pounded on the door and yelled for those inside to let them in. No one answered. Finally, they broke in and stormed into the first room. No one was there. The only items in the room were several huge bags of rice.

The police called out again, but still no one answered. With their pistols drawn, they went into the second room. Huddled in the corner of the room was a family of twelve innocent Vietnamese who spoke no English. They were terrified and had no understanding of why these men with guns had entered their home.

The police discovered their mistake, and in the process, found a family in great need. Fortunately, one of the policemen was a Christian. He knew that he needed to get involved. He knew that it was God who led them there. The policeman became an advocate for refugees and led churches and individuals to become involved with frightened and lonely people often driven from their homeland. Food, friends, and English classes soon changed the future for refugees in this city.

Principle: God is at work where people have need—physical, material, emotional, or spiritual. "Is not this the fast that I choose: to loose the bonds of injustice, to undo the thongs of the yoke, to let the oppressed go free, and to break every yoke? Is it not to share your bread with the hungry, and bring the homeless poor into your house; when you see the naked, to cover them, and not to hide yourself from your own kin? Then your light shall break forth like the dawn, and your healing shall spring up quickly; . . . Then you shall call, and the Lord will answer; you shall cry for help, and he will say, Here I am." (Isa. 58:6–9)

Not only is God concerned with the world around us, He is concerned with the world that is far from us. A friend watched the news and saw multitudes of orphans in Romania. Her heart was moved. She wanted more children, and she had the means by which to care for them. She wondered if God wanted her to adopt a Romanian child. Soon she and her husband traveled to Romania to bring their new daughter home. Before long, her family grew to include not only a Romanian child but also a Chinese child. She found where God was at work and she joined Him there.

"Then the righteous will answer him, 'Lord, when was it that we saw you hungry and gave you food, or thirsty and gave you something to drink? And when was it that we saw you a stranger and welcomed you, or naked and gave you clothing? And when was it we saw you sick or in prison and visited you?' And the king will answer them, 'Truly I tell you, just as you did it to one of the least of these who are members of my family, you did it to me.' " (Matt. 25:37–40)

Principle: The Lord wants you to see where He is at work. He wants you to know His plan. "The Lord works vindication and justice for all who are oppressed. He made known his ways to Moses, his acts to the people of Israel" (Psalm 103:6–7). You and I are His people now. When we are open to seeing, we will see and we will respond.

❧ How Extraordinary People Respond

Responding through Prayer

Karen Felder was preparing for a children's Bible school when she realized that she needed a large amount of Styrofoam to complete one of the activities. She knew that her small church in Colorado did not have the money to purchase what was needed. She went to bed with this concern on her heart. During the night, a strong wind blew. When she awoke in the morning, she discovered a large piece of Styrofoam in her yard leaning against the fence. God knew the desire of her heart, and the Holy Spirit interceded for her. God knows our need before it is voiced and provides all we require for the furthering of His kingdom.

Some years ago, I spent a week in the home of a minister of music and his wife. Each morning before breakfast, the couple used the resources provided by their denomination to pray for people and needs around the world. They interceded for missionaries, for people groups, for the hungry and the thirsty, for those in bondage, and for those enduring persecution. I was moved to see the commitment of this couple to the gospel. As a result of their example, I grew in my understanding of what being an intercessor means.

Do you recall the Lord's heartbreak when He saw that the world lacked intercessors? "The Lord saw it, and it displeased him that there was no justice. He saw that there was no one, and was appalled that there was no one to intervene" (Isa. 59:15–16). Isaiah recorded this observation hundreds of years ago, but I wonder how many intercessors He sees today. Am I one of them? Can the Lord depend on me to stand in the gap for those who have no freedom, no justice, no hope?

I have asked for prayer many times and depended on those whom I asked to follow-through. I depended on their faithfulness to God and their concern for me. At the same time, many have requested prayer from me. Along with their requests, I encountered needs and concerns from within my family, here in my community, and other places for which I know God is looking for praying intercessors.

Intercession is one of the marvelous blessings God has granted to His children. Through intercession, we join Him in what He is doing in individual lives and in the world. God does not intend that our intercession become a burden. Christ promises that when we bear His burden, it will not be heavy. He will carry it with us (Matt. 11:28–30).

The value of intercession is evident in the commitment the prophet Samuel made to God's people to pray for them even when they were making choices that led them away from God. After warning them about their decision, he went on to say, "Moreover as for me, far be it from me that I should sin against the Lord by ceasing to pray for you; and I will instruct you in the good and the right way" (1 Sam. 2:23).

The value of intercession is evident in the apostle Paul's urgent request for prayer for effectiveness and protection in his ministry (2 Thess. 3:1–2). Paul's concern for intercessors is emphasized in that he asked for prayer in several of the letters he wrote to his fellow believers (Eph. 6:19; Col. 4:3–4).

Today you are the intercessor that our Lord is searching for. How can you know you should intercede? First, the Lord's heart broke when He could not find an intercessor. Second, Jesus confirmed the need for prayer in Luke 18:1 when He told the story of a widow who persistently brought her needs before a judge. The judge eventually gave her what she asked because of her persistence. Third, Jesus promised to answer us (Jer. 33:3; John 14:13).

You will be blessed as you become an intercessor; intercession is rewarding. Through prayer, you join God in healing, restoring, redeeming, and freeing persons you know as well as peoples who may live at the ends of the earth.

Prayer Is a Blessing

Prayer is a place of quiet
and a place of song,
a place of still
and a place of activity,
a place of listening
and a place of response,
a place of communion
and a place of fasting,
a place of the spiritual
and a place of the temporal,
a place of humanness
and a place of God.

Prayer is where you wage peace, joy, hope, and faith. Prayer is where your relationship to God becomes active and dynamic as you join Him in the mystery that He has revealed through His Son, Jesus Christ.

As you enter into this awesome blessing of prayer, let me suggest tools that may enhance the journey and provide visual context through which God can reveal opportunities for you to become an intercessor:

- A Bible
- A journal or notebook
- A map of the world
- A map of your community
- Newsletters or bulletins from your church
- A devotional guide
- Letters from missionaries or lists of missionaries and their needs
- Information about various world peoples
- Newspaper articles
- A bulletin board with important reminders for prayer

- A chair
- A place to kneel
- A book for spiritual growth
- Your calendar
- Music of various kinds
- Cassette tapes and videos

Knowing how to intercede requires spending time with God. The quiet of meditation allows God to break through the busyness in your life. He knows the needs for which you can intercede. If you have not learned to take time to listen, try the suggestions of Ann Lipe, a facilitator at the Gettysburg Theological Seminary Festival of the Arts, for contemplative prayer using music.

- Find a quiet, distraction-free place and a comfortable sitting position.
- Notice the present condition of your body and your orientation toward God.
- Listen to a musical selection of your choice.
- Become aware of God's presence in feelings, images, thoughts, and associations evoked by the music.
- Recognize issues or disharmonies in your heart that may be keeping you from receiving what God offers.
- Explore who God is and what He may be inviting you to experience of Him.
- Keep a journal of your thoughts, prayers, Scripture readings, dialogues with God.

Meditation for intercession is most effective when you stay informed and knowledgeable about world needs, missionaries, and peoples of the world. The Lord will speak to you specifics that you may not consider on your own. You will soon be watching and waiting to see the Lord's answers.

Responding through Giving

A young man skied off a cliff, thousands of feet above the valley below. He fell through the air, and at a certain place, he turned his skis to catch an ice-covered ledge, which saved his life. In an interview with a popular sportscaster, the question was asked of him, "Do you have a death wish?" The young man, with a radiant smile, responded, "Oh, no, I don't have a death wish. I have a life wish! I want to live life to the fullest!"

This young man understood that to live life to the fullest you must be willing to give all you have, to live on the edge, to risk it all, to give it all up. Living life to the fullest is found in giving all we have. While most of us are not into extreme sports, we do have a life wish, a desire to live life to the fullest expression of God's power in us. Just as for this young man, it will require that we give all we have.

Giving all, and the blessing received from giving all, is beautifully illustrated in the story of Elijah the prophet and the widow of Zarephath. In response to the evil reign of King Ahab, God told Elijah that the country would suffer severe drought for several years. God's word came true. The drought was so severe that the river from which Elijah drew his water soon dried up. God then told Elijah to go to Zarephath where He had prepared a widow to feed him. Elijah went to Zarephath, found the widow, and asked her to bring him water and food. The widow responded to Elijah's request:

"As the Lord your God lives, I have nothing baked, only a handful of meal in a jar, and a little oil in a jug; I am now gathering a couple of sticks, so that I may go home and prepare it for myself and my son, that we may eat it, and die." (1 Kings 17:12)

The widow explained the life-and-death seriousness of her situation. Elijah responded in a strange way. He told the widow to prepare the food for him rather than for her son and herself.

Why would Elijah make such an unreasonable request? The answer is found in what God had already told Elijah and in the faith Elijah had in God. God had already told Elijah that He had commanded a widow in Zarephath to provide for him. He had not asked her. He had not suggested it to her. He had commanded her. Elijah knew that God's command to this widow was to feed him, and that God's command is always good. Elijah knew that for the widow to live she must be willing to give all she had.

Lesson for giving: Giving is an issue of obedience. God does not request it. He commands it. God settles for nothing less than *all.* "The point is this: the one who sows sparingly will also reap sparingly, and the one who sows bountifully will also reap bountifully. Each of you must give as you have made up your mind, not reluctantly or under compulsion, for God loves a cheerful giver" (2 Cor. 9:6–7).

When Elijah told the widow to feed him first, he also told her the outcome of her obedience. "For thus says the Lord the God of Israel: The jar of meal will not be emptied and the jug of oil will not fail until the day that the Lord sends rain on the earth" (1 Kings 17:14).

The widow did not question or hesitate. I suspect that in her heart, a heart obviously filled with the love of God, she knew God's command when she heard it and she trusted in His promises. Perhaps she had already heard a word from the Lord that had prepared her for this moment. If nothing else, a lifetime of obedience and a lifetime of God's faithfulness had prepared this widow to respond when God asked her to lay all she had on the altar for Him.

All of our lives, we are taught to be reasonable, moderate in all things, not going overboard in any direction. We are guarded in what we say, cautious in our use of time, and careful with our money. We hold on to what we have and find it difficult to part with much. Since moderation is our way of life, we expect those around us to be reasonable in their demands and their expectations of us.

The Christian life is not reasonable. God's requirements of us are unreasonable. He wants all we have and nothing less. He said to Abraham, "I want your beloved son." He said to the widow in the temple, "I want your last mite." He said to Hosea, "I want you to redeem your wife from prostitution, bring her back into your home, and love her." He said to John the Baptist, "I want you to live in the wilderness, forsake all worldly comfort, and preach my word." He said to Mary, "I want you to bear My Son although you are a virgin." He said to Jesus, "I want you to lay down your life for an unworthy people."

Trisa and Brunies are two friends who heard Jesus' command to give all they have and responded. These friends give their time and their money. They are prayer warriors and ministers. They use their gifts and their skills to change lives. In the many years that I have been honored to call them friends, I have been humbled to see the growing desire in their lives to give more and more to God and His mission.

God's demands are not reasonable. What if you give all that you have? Then you have done what God asked of you. God says, "Bring me whatever you have to give, whether it be a few loaves and fishes or abundant gold for the temple."

The widow returned home to prepare her last meal. She first prepared food for Elijah, then for her son and herself. As she mixed the grain with the oil, she depended on God's promise to provide. She worked without resentment, without fear, and without anger. Indeed, her only response was faith.

Lesson for giving: Giving is a faith issue. The widow trusted God enough to give all she had. "And God is able to provide you with every blessing in abundance, so that by always having enough of everything, you may share abundantly in every good work" (2 Cor. 9:8).

Do you believe God can take care of you if you give up your earthly security? Money? Home? Time? In one of the poorest nations of our world, a colony of lepers living in poverty each year takes an offering for world missions. A successful lawyer in Colorado gave up a six-figure salary and sold most of his possessions in order to go as a mission volunteer. A family on a limited income used their vacation time and extra cash each year to help build churches. Lepers, a lawyer, and a family are people of great faith giving all they have.

Strengthened by faith, the widow of Zarephath prepared the first meal for Elijah. Afterward, she prepared a meal for her son and then herself. Do you remember the outcome?

"She went and did as Elijah said, so that she as well as he and her household ate for many days. The jar of meal was not emptied, neither did the jug of oil fail, according to the word of the Lord that he spoke by Elijah." (1 Kings 17:15–16)

Until you give all you have, you cannot receive all the blessings God wants to give. Most of us settle for what we have on hand, thinking that if we hang on to this we can still have more of what God offers. It does not work that way. The widow had other choices. She could have said to Elijah, "I'm sorry, but my first obligation is to my child. I'll pray for you to find food." She and her child would have eaten that last meal, only to wait for death to come.

A widow's obedience and faith brought blessing that was supernatural. Her faith allowed God to bless her beyond reason with meal and oil that did not run out even in a time of drought. God showed this widow His great love for her by filling her life with His gracious mercies. Surely you also have heard the Lord calling to you, "Give this up so I can show you how much I love you. I have something far better that I long to give you."

Lesson for giving: Giving is an issue of blessings. If you give all you have, you will receive God's great blessings. "You will be enriched in every way for your great generosity, which will produce thanksgiving to God through us" (2 Cor. 9:11).

God's love for you is so great that He chose to give you everything—His own life through His most beloved Son, Jesus. "Greater love has no one than this, that one lay down his life for his friends" (John 15:13 NASB). In God's case, He laid down His life for *more* than His friends. He laid down His life for you, you who were His enemy until you turned from your sin. You might say that God loves you unreasonably.

God loves you even though you are unworthy. He knows that you have nothing of value on your own. Even so, He offers to bless you with the riches of heaven, but the storehouses of your life must be emptied of all worldly garbage before God will pour into your life the abundance of His good blessings. God longs to give you that which is far better than anything to which you might choose to cling.

What does He ask in return? His only request is that your love for Him be likewise unreasonable. People who give all they have are people who love unreasonably. People who love unreasonably have a love big enough to embrace the entire world. They are the people who love the world as God loves the world.

What if you give all you have? The Scriptures say that "The jar of meal was not emptied, neither did the jug of oil fail, according to the word of the Lord that he spoke by Elijah" (1 Kings 17:16). When you give all you have, a wonderful thing happens. Then and only then can God pour into your life the abundant, unreasonable blessings that will enable you to experience life to the fullest.

Responding through Ministering

Granny Sapp went to her pastor and said, "God wants me to make puppets." As a result of that commitment, Granny Sapp's puppets have been used in ministries all around the world; sailors have come to Christ and hurting children have been comforted.

Linda was buying groceries when she saw a family struggling to understand the English words on the cans and boxes. She assisted them, and as a result, began an internationals ministry in her church.

Trisa told the women in her church that the school for preschoolers with special needs was looking for volunteers to assist a few hours each day. The women realized that their involvement in this ministry would express God's love to the community and to the families of these little ones. Several women volunteered. As a result, a number of families came to Christ.

Ministry is one way that we join God in His redeeming activity. Think for a moment about your life. First of all, you were created in God's image. He gave you His potential for giving, loving, forgiving, caring, and holiness. Sin came into your life, but in Christ you were redeemed. Your redemption allowed God to continue the process of creation in you so that you will be remade in the likeness of Christ. God's creation process is multiplied as your ministry results in others coming to know God's redemption.

God has planned for you to become a redeeming person, redeeming persons from sin, poverty, bondage, oppression, sickness, hunger, and other needs of humanity. Jesus calls us to follow His example of ministry. Remember what He did for His disciples and for hurting people in His life? He fed them. He healed them. He encouraged them. He taught them. He restored them. He served them.

Jesus is looking for people who will serve as He served, who will wash the feet of those who are tired, cook for those who are hungry, and go to those who are rejected. God has equipped us to serve by giving us the many gifts we have discussed in this book. Our personalities, skills, talents, gifts, God's character, time, money, experiences—everything we have prepares us to follow Christ's example of service. The combination of these wonderful gifts with our service is what we call *ministry.*

You are a minister and through you, lives will be changed as you serve with the blessings God has already poured into your life. Have you considered:

• Rocking AIDS babies
• Conducting Bible schools in migrant camps
• Doing housing repair for the elderly
• Tutoring students
• Offering your home for after school care
• Cleaning the home of an ill neighbor
• Shopping for a homebound single
• Cooking in a community food program
• Working in a shelter for the homeless
• Helping teachers in the school system
• Encouraging workers in the malls or other public businesses
• Mentoring a woman who is seeking to rebuild her life
• Becoming a grandparent to a lonely child

What a delightful invitation we have—to hold a small face in our hands and wipe away a tear, to put an arm around an elderly woman needing to be touched, to teach a group of homeless women how to interview for a job, or to mentor a young mother in taking care of her new baby. Aren't these the serendipities of life, where we discover an unexpected joy and blessing?

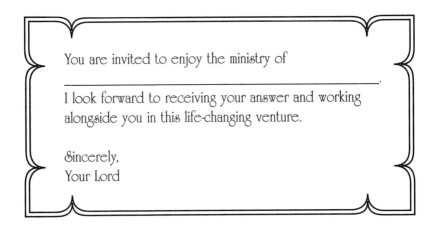

You are invited to enjoy the ministry of

_____.

I look forward to receiving your answer and working alongside you in this life-changing venture.

Sincerely,
Your Lord

What ministry is God writing in the blank space on your invitation?

Responding through Witnessing

One week on the television news show, *Good Morning, America*, weatherman Tony Perkins went on location to work in different vocations each day. The first day that I watched, Tony was a rock star. On another day, he worked as a steeplejack. Viewers had written to suggest different vocations. They wanted Tony to identify with them in their everyday lives.

Tony's behavior provided an interesting contrast in the two sessions I watched. While he welcomed the role of rock star, he did not enjoy the work of the steeplejack. Though he delighted in the admiration of the cheering crowd at the concert, he did not relish hanging far above the ground while being held in place with ropes, chains, and bracing. You could see the fun he had as a rock star, but you could not miss the fear in his eyes as a steeplejack.

Even so, I have to commend Tony for stepping out of his comfort zone to identify with someone from another work culture. Tony responded like most of us. We find it easy to identify with the people whose lives we consider appealing. On the other hand, identifying with those who are different or whose lives we do not understand or accept can be much more challenging.

Identifying with those who are different is exactly what the apostle Paul did to share God's love with the people around him. He broke out of his comfort zone. You might think this is a wild idea, the thought of trying to put aside personal preferences so others can know God. Was this Paul's idea, or was it God's? The truth is that it started with God Himself. A favorite song of mine, "God Still Loves the World," begins like this:

In a day when the world was so much younger,
there came to earth a promised man;
so the love of God could walk among the people,
who would see Him live and die, and live again.

("God Still Loves the World" written by Billy Blackwood and Gordon Jensen © 1986 One Story Music and Word Music, Inc. All Rights Reserved. Used by Permission. International Rights Secured.)

God identified with a people whose lives were as far from His love, grace, compassion, righteousness, and holiness as east is from the west. He did this out of love.

"God's love was revealed among us in this way: God sent his only Son into the world so that we might live through him. In this is love, not that we loved God but that he loved us and sent His Son to be the atoning sacrifice for our sins." (1 John 4:9–10)

God came to earth and identified with us by becoming human. That is why Jesus lived on earth and experienced all that we experience. He became human so He could show us how to live. His life was an example of how we could identify with others so they could know God's love. We who believe in Jesus as Lord and Savior have done so because God loved us enough to identify with us right where we are. For the most part, He identified with us through the ministry and witness of those around us—parents, friends, teachers, coworkers, pastors—others who give life to the Word of God, revealing God in everyday terms.

Jesus identified with people. The song I mentioned earlier goes on to say:

God loved the world when Jesus blessed the children,
When his touch became the blind man's time to see.
On that ancient afternoon, they crucified him,
His love became the greatest fact in history.

Think of examples of Jesus identifying with people. What others do you recall that I have not listed?

- Jesus identified with people when He met a woman at the well and asked for a drink of water.
- Jesus identified with people when He lived without home or security.
- Jesus identified with people when He called a tax collector down from a tree and went to his home.
- Jesus identified with people when He took time for the crippled, the blind, the lonely.
- Jesus identified with people when He washed the feet of His friends.
- Jesus identified with people when from the cross He cared for His grieving mother.
- Jesus identified with people when He met the apostle Paul on His way to work, showing him a better way than the road he had chosen.

Even the great apostle Paul needed to see God's love in a way that he could understand. So God identified with Paul right where he was, on his way to work.

Understanding what it means for us to identify with others

is easier if we recall that when Jesus chose to identify with us, He gave up all his rights as the Son of God, King of kings, Lord of lords. He did that for Paul. He did that for you. He did that for me.

Asking an American to give up her rights is like asking a fish to live without water. We believe we deserve whatever rights we have. The apostle Paul had the same struggle, and in writing to his fellow Christians in Corinth, he defended his rights. Then he went on to say:

"Nevertheless, we have not made use of this right, but we endure anything rather than put an obstacle in the way of the gospel of Christ." (1 Cor. 9:12)

Paul's experience with Christ freed him to give up his rights for a greater right, the right to proclaim the good news of God's love. When Paul was able to put aside his personal rights for a greater right, he also was able to join Christ in identifying with people who needed to know God's love. Paul went on to write:

"To the weak I became weak, so that I might win the weak. I have become all things to all people, that I might by all means save some. I do it all for the sake of the gospel, so that I may share in its blessings." (1 Cor. 9:22–23)

Paul listed some of the rights he had forsaken for a greater right. As you read these, what rights are you ready to lay aside to identify with lost and hurting people who live around you?

- Paul was free to live as an honored Roman citizen, but he lived as a despised Jew.
- Paul was free from the burden of the Law, but he lived by the Law so that those who were still bound by the Law would be willing to hear God's message.

- Paul was freed by Christ's law, but he became as one outside the law to build a bridge to the gospel.
- Paul was free to live with pure conscience, but to the weak he became weak so those who were easily wounded would find confidence and hope in Christ.

At every point Paul identified himself with others, and illustrated the truth that the gospel cannot be preached except as you and I are willing to take our place beside those whom we would win. Paul's life proved that he was willing to do whatever was required.

- Paul was willing to be God's fool. "We are fools for the sake of Christ, but you are wise in Christ" (1 Cor. 4:10).
- Paul was willing to forsake pride and ego. "We are weak, but you are strong. You are held in honor, but we in disrepute" (1 Cor. 4:10).
- Paul was willing to deny self. "To the present hour we are hungry and thirsty, we are poorly clothed and beaten and homeless, and we grow weary from the work of our own hands. When reviled, we bless; when persecuted, we endure; when slandered, we speak kindly. We have become like the rubbish of the world, the dregs of all things, to this very day" (1 Cor. 4:11–13).

Paul gave up his personal rights and freedoms for a greater freedom, to become a slave to Christ and to his fellow human beings. Paul said, "I am willing to do whatever it takes." Willing, willing, willing. Over and over again, because Paul was willing, God identified with people through Paul's life.

God works in the same way today. I was in Denver, Colorado, with several thousand teenagers for a millennial celebration. At seven sites around the United States, all of them linked by satellite, thousands of teenagers celebrated the coming of a new millennium. The entire event was a high-energy experience; but on the first night, a Christian rock band that was high noise and high adrenaline led the worship. Seated in front of me were a middle-aged couple and their group of about a dozen teens.

The couple was not accustomed to the type of music we were hearing. When they saw the response of their youth, however, they joined in, clapping their hands and lifting their voices to the Lord. Who knows how God will work in the lives of those teenagers because a middle-aged couple said, "We are willing to become all things to all people by all means so we can save some."

You may be wondering how "by all means" interprets for your lifestyle. Here are some guidelines to use as you think about how you will identify "by all means" for the cause of the gospel.

- Nothing is out of bounds if it honors God.
- Building the bridge to another human is always the goal.
- Every talent, skill, gift, ability, resource that you have is just for this—by all means.
- It will take all means to win some.
- Jesus used all means and still won only some.
- The fewer means we use, the fewer will be won.
- Surely God intends that all the means we have at our disposal are to be used up for His purposes.

Dr. Joy Neal equips persons to participate in a national telephone evangelism response ministry. Persons who want to know more about Christ call an 800 number that rings through to someone who is trained to share their faith in Christ. Joy tells of one volunteer who has witnessed for Christ to many persons through this ministry, some deeply hurting and looking for hope. She has even been confronted by a person claiming to be the devil, to which she responded, "So you know who Jesus

Christ is. And you know the words He has spoken to you." She said that when the name of Jesus was mentioned, the person hung up. As a volunteer, she has discovered that God empowers His people when they are willing to use all means to share their faith in Him.

Joy also tells of a 13-year-old girl who called the evangelism response number and received Christ. When the volunteer asked her how she had heard about the number, her response was, "I didn't see it anywhere, I just called 1-800-Jesus." When we remember that God is the initiator of a person's hunger for Him, we will gladly participate in an evangelism response ministry, church visitation ministry, go next door to a neighbor, or travel to a place where the people have never heard of Christ's love. We will be willing to live in ways that reveal who God is. We will become more intentional about becoming and being all that we need to be for the sake of the gospel.

Using every means available is an intentional decision. Rachel Scott, one of the young women I've mentioned in a previous chapter, understood this. She died in the Columbine High School shooting in 1999. From all that has been told of her, it appears that she had made an intentional decision to use every means at her disposal to share Christ through her life. She mimed a song telling of the sacrifice of Christ for her drama class. She stopped by the road to hold an umbrella over a man who was changing a flat tire in the rain. She prayed for boldness and shared Christ with her friends. Her classmates commented on her kindness. Rachel was only sixteen years old, but she used all means to identify with others for the cause of the gospel.

Rachel's life is proof that to use all means you do not have to be a theologian or have the Bible memorized, or have 30 years of Christian experience. All you need is love for the world that comes from loving God who first loved you.

Responding through Volunteering

The September day that my department worked on a Habitat for Humanity home just happened to be one of the hottest days of the year. We met on site, looking pretty cute in our matching volunteer T-shirts. By the end of the day, the fact that we had been working and sweating like construction workers was obvious.

In the beginning, none of us knew how we could make a contribution. Yet we came prepared with paint brushes, paint rollers, gloves, hats, hammers, and other tools. The crew chief told us what had to be done. After prayer we were off to work.

That particular day, two needs rose to the top. One was for volunteers to do *cornering*. That meant reaching over our heads to paint the top edge of the wall below the ceiling. It meant painting every edge and every corner. The other need was for someone to scrape from the floor the plaster chunks glued to it and then to sweep the place clean.

Our team went to work, taking breaks now and then for water and cookies and a sandwich at lunch. The outside awning with a fan blowing in it was a welcome relief after working inside the hot house all day.

By the end of the day, we and other volunteers had cornered and painted all the rooms, completed the roofing, cleaned the floor, and prepared the house for carpeting. We achieved what the crew chief needed done that day. The only mistake we made was taking a photo of our team later in the day, instead of when we first arrived. With our sweaty hair, paint-covered clothes, and dirty faces, we looked like a work crew for sure!

The best part of the day was meeting the woman who would be living in the house with her children and brother. We celebrated with her the new life she would soon begin in her new home. Her joy and humble acceptance of this gift that had come her way moved all of us.

Volunteering always blesses the volunteer more than anyone

else. Using whatever we have to touch another life brings a built-in reward that only God could have ordained as part of the human experience.

A few days ago, my friend Laura returned from prayer-walking and helping with a retreat for women in Bosnia. She is aware of the peoples who live in that country and the horrible loss of lives and homes that resulted from a ravaging war. Last year she prayerwalked in countries where people groups have little access to the gospel of Jesus Christ. The more she serves as a volunteer, the greater her desire to serve again.

Now, because of the Internet, you can access information about people groups around the world. Some are struggling with poverty, war, and oppression. All need to know the message of Christ. You can learn about projects and ministries sponsored by organizations who need people to invest their time in helping to meet needs and share Christ. Your church may have volunteer projects or need volunteers in ministries right there in your own community.

Many missionaries around the world also depend on volunteers to help accomplish the tasks needed to reach the people where they serve. One missionary wrote, "Volunteers are some of God's choicest servants. They provide skills that may be lacking in the missionary family. They may bring fresh ideas for ministry opportunities and serve as couriers for needed supplies. They become sources of encouragement during challenging times in the lives of missionaries."

Responding through Learning

Ruth Todd came to the podium in the morning worship service. The minister who coordinates volunteers in the church introduced Ruth and told of her involvement in ministry to homeless women and their children. Then he asked, "Ruth, how did you become involved in this ministry?"

Ruth responded by telling of her involvement with a group

of women in her church who come together each month to learn about the needs of the world and how God is at work through His people. Almost ten years ago, her group studied the needs of the homeless and knew that they needed to know more about the homeless in their own city.

One of the women in the group worked with the social services in the city and knew of a shelter where homeless women could stay until they found jobs and got their own places to live. The women in the group called the shelter and asked if they could come for a visit. They are still going to the shelter nearly ten years later. The women and children who stay there can hardly wait for the volunteers to arrive for they always bring activities, snacks, fellowship, and an encouraging word from the Lord. Not only do they minister in the shelter, they assist women in getting household items they need as they move into their own housing.

Filling our minds with God's concerns and God's plan increases our responsiveness when opportunities to touch lives come our way. God wants us to know His plan and how He is working it out. Ephesians 1 reminds us that God has let us in on the plan so we can join Him in what He is doing. John 1:15 tells us that Jesus has told us everything about what God is doing so we would be His friends and come along beside Him in His work. Amos 3:7 confirms that God intends that His chosen people know what He is up to.

Both New Testament and Old call for God's people to open their eyes and be mentally alert to the signs of the time. No "out" is offered for believers who choose to turn a deaf ear and blind eye to the work of God in the world.

You might be surprised if you were to examine all the times that you met a need. How did you know about those needs? Did a friend tell you? Did you read about them in a newsletter or the newspaper? Did your church announce them in worship sessions or through the church bulletin? Every need you have met was in some way communicated to you before you could respond.

Our love for God puts within us a growing hunger to know more about His work so we can be more active in serving with Him through prayer, through giving, through ministry, and through telling the good news of God's love in Jesus Christ.

The Extraordinary Work of God

Where virtue replaces sin,
Where peace replaces war,
Where joy replaces sorrow,
Where life replaces death,
Where truth replaces deceit,
Where justice replaces wrong,
Where freedom replaces bondage,
Where satisfaction replaces hunger and thirst,
Where giving replaces getting,
Where open doors replace closed ones,
Where mercy replaces vengeance,
Where reconciliation replaces schism,
Where hope replaces despair,
Where love replaces hate.

Live The Extraordinary

The invitation's open;
Jesus leads the way.
It's time to enjoy the fragrance
That comes from His parade.
The bands are playing to His praise,
All restraints are thrown aside.
Take His hand to live today,
With Jesus as your guide.

Chapter Twelve

Everyday Steps for the Extraordinary Journey

Unexpected pleasures,
Unanticipated joy,
Unknown but now known friends,
Undiscovered but now uncovered life,
Unseen but now seen . . .
Hope.

I saw her wandering in the hallway. The look of quiet desperation could not be missed. Her eyes were red. She paced the floor as though she were running out of time. I tried casual conversation, but she responded with very few words. "Can I help you?" I finally offered. By then, we were facing each other at the end of the hallway. Long seconds passed without a word, the eyes of two strangers becoming friends. "I'm trying to decide if I can trust you," she said. I explained that I did not mean to pry, but she continued, "I tried to kill myself the night before last. This morning I shot myself up with drugs before I came here. The women I came with do not know what I've done."

I wasn't prepared for her words. *I'm not a counselor!* I cried within. *I should have stayed in my conference room preparing for the next session*, I thought, but I was all she had. So God reached through me to her. Her journey has been long and is not over yet. Time in drug rehab, repentance for a crime, a season in prison, and a family in pain made the journey turbulent. God and His children have kept her moving toward completion. Women in her church are keeping her on the path that God had already planned.

Extraordinary living is practical and relevant to the world around us. As Bob Sjogren states in his book, *Unveiled at Last* (YWAM, 1992), the believer's life has a top line and a bottom line. The top line is God's blessing for His people. The bottom line is that "He wants His people to not only enjoy that blessing, but then to turn around and be a blessing to all families on the face of the earth, resulting in His greater glory." Extraordinary living embraces both the top and bottom line of God's plan.

Where do we find and experience the extraordinary life? What can we do to bring the spiritual nature of our lives to actuality in our daily routines? In thinking about my own experience, I have discovered that God invites me to go fishing with Him on a regular basis. The only problem is that He often extends His invitation when the sky is full of clouds, the water is turbulent, or the rest of the crew has yet to show up. I assume that this just is not the best time to go fishing, that the risk is too high, and I find it hard to say "yes." I feel too alone, and I know that I do not have the support needed to stay safe. The last thing I want to do is try something new or make a change. I wish I were someone else, anyone else, who is braver and truer.

Fortunately, I *have* accepted God's invitation at times, even when the sky was dark and the waves were high. I *have* discovered options, but they are options that I must use over and over each step of the way with my extraordinary God. Is God asking you to go fishing? He wants each of us to fish for other people, inviting them into His kingdom. Try my options, and let's get going! Life is being lived right now!

›‹ *Take a Risk*

A six-year-old girl was seated next to me on the plane. "I've never been on a plane before," she said. "I am going to visit my aunt." The plane began to taxi down the runway. The little girl looked up at me and asked, "May I hold your hand?" I took her soft tiny hand in mine, gave her a hug, and off we flew into the sky. We held hands all the way to Kentucky, talking and laughing, looking out the window, visiting with the flight attendant, and having a delightful time. Before we knew it, the plane was landing. The little girl ran to her cousins' arms. Her fears were gone. I have no doubt that when she flies home she will be much more excited about her journey on an airplane.

The sooner we try the unknown, the sooner we will have the rejuvenating experience of turning to God and asking, "May I hold Your hand?" When we risk following God, we never go alone. In fact, I am convinced that what *appears* as a risk is not a risk at all when God is leading the way.

When Jesus came walking on the water, Peter longed to join Him, to know His Lord was really there. Jesus invited Peter to join Him, but Peter became frightened. He began to sink in the water. "[Peter] cried out, 'Lord, save me!' Jesus immediately reached out his hand and caught him, saying to him, 'You of little faith, why did you doubt?' " (Matt. 14:30–31).

Risk that new job, risk speaking to the new neighbor, risk

moving to a far away place, risk a major change in lifestyle. Some risk will always be in God's plan for you. Until you risk, you will never know the awesome faithfulness of our God.

❧ Say Yes

Every night of the revival at my home church in Wyoming, I felt God's Spirit urging me to make a commitment of special service. I did not move because I felt unworthy. Every night, I discussed my insecurity with God. Finally, the week was over. What a relief! When I left for vacation to visit my parents in Oklahoma a few days later, I felt sure that God had changed His mind about wanting me.

The urging and the agony did not stop. At my parents' church, I struggled through three Sunday morning and evening services. During every service, I gripped the pew in front of me to steady my hands and heart. The presence of God was so powerful that I literally had a physical sense of His call. Still I struggled with my unworthiness.

On the last night of my visit, I was seated at the back of the large sanctuary beside my parents and my daughter. The urging became more profound than ever before. I knew I had to do something. I asked God to help me with this decision.

The new pastor led a closing invitation. Many people went forward, but not me. Finally the pastor said, "This will be the last verse we will sing, and the invitation will close." Since the invitation had closed, I felt safe in praying, "Lord, if you want me to go forward, then lead the pastor to ask for one more verse of invitation." No sooner had I prayed this prayer than the pastor said, "I feel led that we should sing one more verse of invitation." I nearly fainted when I heard that. Still I did not go. I pleaded with God to help me.

I pleaded, "Lord, help me. My family knows how imperfect I am. How can you call me?" I knew I would have to walk past my parents to get to the aisle, and they knew me so well. Would they believe that God could call me?

About that time, my mother and father went forward and made a commitment of their own. I could not believe what I was seeing. I knew that God had reached out to me in His infinite mercy, removing every obstacle that I perceived to be in my way of saying "yes" to Him. I took my daughter's hand and nearly ran to the front of the sanctuary. That night I said yes to God's call to special ministry, not knowing what an extraordinary life waited on the other side of the gate that He had opened.

As for my parents, they have been some of my greatest supporters. They have blessed my ministry in more ways than I can ever repay. They have gone with me to events, heard me speak, and sat in my conferences. They have spoken encouraging words when I needed them and shared their wisdom when asked.

Moses offered numerous excuses to the Lord before he said yes. Barak insisted on the presence of Deborah before he would say yes. Jeremiah explained to God that he was too young before he said yes. Paul kicked against the pricks of the Holy Spirit before he finally said yes.

On the other hand, a woman named Lydia did not hesitate to say yes to beginning the first church in Macedonia. An unknown woman did not hesitate to say yes to honoring Jesus with the washing of His feet with her tears and her hair. A woman in Samaria, when encountering Jesus by a well, did not hesitate to say yes.

So I say to you, say yes to God. If He is asking anything of you, your obedience will lead into a lifetime of praise for His mercies.

❧ Join a Group

A few summers ago, I participated in a women's group focused on mentoring. The group was small, and I went to the first few sessions before beginning a busy summer of travel. I received notes from the leader and other women in the group. I had lunch with several of the women and became acquainted with women in my church that I had not known well.

The next year, the leader of our group was killed in a car accident. She had mentored many in her work as a university administrator. Her death left a huge gap in many hearts. How glad I was that I had come to know her gentle caring spirit through that group experience.

Even the prophet Elijah was afraid when he thought he was the only one who loved God. If Elijah needed others, then we certainly do also. Do you remember the story of Lydia? She prayed by the river with other women who loved God. In my work with women, I have discovered that women who belong to groups are often more actively involved in God's work than those who are loners. The joy of traveling to a distant country is multiplied when surrounded by a team of volunteers. The challenge of keeping a ministry going is manageable when we share the load with others of God's servants. The skills and talents needed to accomplish a task are more likely to be found in a group rather than in one single individual.

Groups are places where you can find new friends, develop support systems, gain accountability for living to please God, and risk going into the hard places of life where you might never go alone. Not only that, the celebration of success is certainly more fun when shared with others who also understand the marvelous working of God among His people.

❧ *Enlist a Prayer Partner*

When I became the state director for our women's mission organization in Wyoming, two retired professional women from Alabama came to assist me with training. I fell in love with Brunies and Miriam. They became my prayer partners, an extended family in Alabama. We stayed in touch through calls and letters, never dreaming that one day I would live in Alabama, too.

A few years ago Miriam died, but I knew that I could depend on her prayers until the end. Now my relationship with Brunies is ever more precious, and I know that I can share with her any need for faithful and concerted prayer. Every day I go forth assured that she is praying for me.

I have several friends in my life that count on my prayers for them. I have enjoyed seeing God work in their lives through the years. The bond of our prayer relationship has seen us through separation, difficulties, and misunderstandings. It has provided numerous joys and deepened trust and love.

Every believer needs to build a spiritual fortress around her life. One friend suggested that we should each have at least eight people committed to praying for our families and ourselves. Prayer partners are a gift from God. We can talk with them and cry with them. We can rejoice with them and change the world with them.

Enlisting people who will be prayer warriors for us is essential for we are in a spiritual war, and spiritual wars are fought through prayer. When we understand this, we can love others. We can reach out and open ourselves to others for the sake of prayer. As our trust grows, we can discover that we are more accepting of others and more accepting of ourselves.

ஆ Be Yourself

When my sister and I were young, we enjoyed pretending to be someone else. Since we moved often, we sometimes arrived in a new community and decided to have an English accent as long as we could. I do not think that ever lasted long, but we thought we were pretty hot stuff in our affected roles.

Most of us have those times when we wish we could be someone other than who we really are. In reality, most people are interested in knowing the *real* you. We are not attracted for long to people who wear masks, for we are never sure of who they are and how they really feel about who we are.

Even if we were to try to hide our real selves, we cannot keep it up for long. I have noticed when I've interviewed people for positions that I have a sense of who they are regardless of what they say. Usually, if someone's inner voice tells her something that contradicts what she is seeing, she will soon discover that the inner voice was more on target than perhaps she was even willing to acknowledge.

One reality of being ourselves is that people are less likely to be disappointed in us. We are who we say we are, and we act as expected from the beginning. A consistency in life takes shape. When we choose godliness, then our real selves become more and more beautiful in behavior and attitude.

Rhonda Kelley speaks of godliness in her book, *A Woman's Guide to Personal Holiness.* She encourages readers to develop holy habits, habits that are pure in thought and deed. When we choose to be holy, the real self is easier and easier to be because we like it more and more. Our personal holiness is directly linked to the ease with which we reveal our true selves.

Being yourself is extraordinary. Seeing what God can do through and with you is the joy of your relationship to Him. When we experience the transformation God makes of our lives, we see Him as ever more worthy of worship, praise, honor, and glory.

❧ Try Something New

While many complete college right after high school, I did it the hard way and finished college when my *daughter* was in high school. As a more mature student, I did well. I felt pretty good about my studies as I reached the last term. Then I realized that I needed a senior level class, and I also needed an art class. I took a senior level art class in layout. What a class it was. We had a room full of skilled artists . . . and me. I will never forget the day I turned in my T-shirt design. My professor could hardly keep from laughing in hysteria. He said, "Andrea, would you let me re-do this for you so you can complete your layout assignment?"

Honestly, my T-shirt design was really bad. Even so, I learned the language and techniques of layout, and I have used that skill many times since I completed the class.

The point of learning something new is not to be good at it, but to discover what you are good at. I cannot imagine that there are many things we could learn as we follow God's lead that will not enhance our lives or our knowledge of who we are.

❧ Make a Change

After twenty-plus years of marriage, Sandi Rives and her husband Jim decided to make a needed change in their home. They wanted to change the dining room. When she told me they were making changes, I assumed she meant redecorating. Forget that! They decided to move the dining room into the living room and the living room into the dining room. Redecorating was just part of the change they would make to accomplish their intended purpose. Since Sandi's spiritual gift is hospitality, I suspect that this change is a direct result of their desire to make their home even more accommodating for baby showers and other customary activities in their routine.

Even small changes in our routines, customs, or lifestyles can cause increased stress. Therefore, many of us avoid change. We may consider moving our dining room to the living room, but we are often afraid to actually make the move. Will it work? Do I have the ability to do this? Will I be able to afford it once I get started? How will others feel about this? Will I like it when I am finished? If you are a person who is most comfortable with a low stress environment and change is what you like least in the world, then you would deserve applause for moving your dining room to your living room.

Several years ago, I attended a workshop led by a psychologist who tested our stress comfort level. The test began with a list of statements. We checked the ones that were most like us. On a piece of paper were three horizontal lines, one above the other. Each line had *least* written at the left end and *most* written at the right end. The bottom line was titled *low stress,* the middle was *average stress,* the top was *high stress.*

The psychologist asked us to total the number of statements we checked and then place the number on one of the lines. Line one listed numbers 1–10; so if you had checked only one statement, you placed an X on the bottom line at the end that said *least.* This meant that you were most comfortable when you have no stress in your life. You would find it difficult to deal with any type of change at work, at home, or at play.

Line two listed the numbers 11–20 on it while the top line had 21–30. If you had thirty statements checked, then you put your X on the top line at the end marked *most.* That meant you love stress and spend your vacations sky diving and racing cars. You are one of the daredevils of our world. You might jump the Grand Canyon on a motorcycle, for instance.

I brought the test home so Mike and I could take it together. Although both our scores fell on the middle continuum, Mike was at the *least* end, and I was at the *most* end. He enjoys a life of moderately low stress while I prefer living on the edge of high risk.

Change is often compared to risk. If we are hesitant to risk, we may be hesitant to change. Each of us responds differently to the idea of stepping into the unknown. When Mike makes a change, it is usually with much deliberation and does not happen quickly. I, on the other hand, am more likely to make the change just for the excitement and anticipation of change itself. Of course, the change I enjoy the most is the change I initiate or that I control.

Regardless of our comfort level, the Christian story is a story of continual change. For us, there is no such thing as static or stationary. We move forward in our commitment and spiritual growth, or we fall behind. Read the Bible through this year and see how much change the Lord continually required of His people. Today's Christian life is no different. We are asked to change, and then change again, and then again, as we know more of God with each disturbance in our routine.

Some Christians have made radical lifestyle changes as they became more like Christ. They forsook homes or left high-paying salaries to serve in a nonprofit organization. They became foster parents or prison chaplains. They moved to the inner city where the numbers and needs of the lost are growing with each passing day. They became advocates for people whom society has forgotten. Tom Sine, author of *Mustard Seed Versus McWorld*, challenges believers to completely rethink their lifestyles and embrace "whole-life discipleship and stewardship in which we reinvent how we use time and money to put God's purposes first in every area of life."

You are changing every day. The joy of it all is that God has freed you to choose only the things that take you to abundant life. You have the freedom to give every change to God for His empowering blessing. Get ready! Change is coming. You are invited to become more like Christ every day, step-by-step on the journey of extraordinary living!

Chapter Thirteen

From the Mundane to the Extraordinary

On the edge of the world,
A glow begins to form, yellow and orange and pink,
So small . . .
It could go unnoticed.
Too much to do, no time to stay?
Don't walk away to never see
The brilliance of the coming day.

The sun never catches up with God. Here it is, still dark, and God's voice calls me. My friends who are not morning people would agree that God never sleeps, for He speaks to them in the late hours of the day and night. The leap from mundane to extraordinary is found in the early morning hours, the late night hours, and all the hours in between. God does not rest. He is always available. He has a message for you that will transform your life from mundane to extraordinary.

Are you into computer games? If so, you may have discovered that some games allow you one way through with no shortcuts. I have one game that drives me to frustration. The program will not allow the player to find the goal without solving each puzzle along the journey. I have to use every hint available to make any headway.

Extraordinary living is not a game, but neither does it offer any shortcuts. *Prayer* and *Bible study* are the two pieces of the puzzle that must be used throughout the journey, no matter how long the journey may be. The ways, times, approaches, places, and resources are limitless; but prayer and Bible study, however, wherever, and whenever you choose are the muscles in your jump from the mundane to the extraordinary. Have you tried any shortcuts, like reading books other than the Bible or filling your time with church activities?

Shortcuts are not in God's game plan. Apart from prayer and Bible study, you will miss out on the fullness of God's revelation, God's transformation, God's revolution, God's power, and God's delight—a simple plan with extraordinary results.

ॐ *God's Revelation*

"But, as it is written, 'What no eye has seen, nor ear heard, nor the human heart conceived, what God has prepared for those who love him'—these things God has revealed to us through the Spirit; for the Spirit searches everything, even the depths of God" (1 Cor. 2:9–10).

Evelyn Christensen explained in a recent article how God has been involved in every book she has written. She described her dining room table laden with piles of manuscript pages and notes for an upcoming book. Evelyn told how God revealed Himself to her over and over again.

> "Every word on every one of those pieces of paper had come directly from Him. That's how all my books have been written—in my prayer closet with God.
> "How does that work? It actually is very simple. I just have to listen. For many years I have spent two hours, and often more, in the wee hours of the night just with God—opening my heart for Him to be in control of our communicating.
> "In these precious times, He recalls scripture I have hidden in my heart recently or years before and interweaves them into current specific answers. He reveals awesome new thoughts to me from His omniscient mind; or He suddenly unfolds an outline for future or tomorrow's speaking—or for a point in the book. Then I grab my note pad from my night stand, and immediately write down what He has said." (from *Something More, A Publication of Christian Women United*)

Revelation is more than the last book in the Bible. Revelation is a profound doctrine, a theological reality. Revelation is all that God does to make Himself known to us. Revelation is God's activity of self-disclosure. He wants us to know Him. He wants us to know His character, His plan, and His view of who we are. When you choose to give yourself to God, you are responding to what God has already initiated.

Revelation is the expected behavior of a giving God. "Come, talk with me," He urges. "Experience Me for yourself. Get to know Me intimately. I have nothing to hide from you. I am willing to reveal to you all that you are willing to receive." God is a giving God, and He chooses to give Himself away to you. He wants you to know Him more intimately than you know your child, your spouse, or your earthy parents. He wants you to be more intimate with Him than you are with any human being.

A small calendar on my desk asks this question: "Have you looked at a night sky recently and allowed yourself to feel the wonder of its vastness?" The vastness of the night sky becomes at once more amazing and more understood when you are familiar with the science of astronomy. The vastness of God becomes both awe-inspiring and more personal through prayer and Bible study. Jennifer Kennedy Dean writes in her book *Riches Stored in Secret Places,* "The Spirit, working directly in your mind and understanding, discloses deeper levels of truth. First Corinthians 2:12 tells you that God has given you His Spirit for this purpose: 'that [you] might understand what God has freely given [you].' Because you have the Holy Spirit, you can understand what the human intellect alone is unable to comprehend."

Try a brief exercise. Lay this book aside and turn in your Bible to Psalm 33. What do you read about God that is awe-inspiring or that speaks of His vastness? What do you read that makes Him more personal? Take time to praise God aloud for what you read of His character in verses 4 and 5. Praise Him for what you read of His power in verses 6–9. Praise Him for what you read about His sovereignty over the entire world in verses 10–17. Praise Him for what you read of His salvation in verses 18–19. Now ask God to reveal to you what He wants you to learn from this wonderful psalm. Be silent. Listen. Write what He says to you here:

_____

_____

_____

_____

_____

_____

&. God's Transformation

"So if anyone is in Christ, there is a new creation: everything old has passed away; see, everything has become new!" (2 Cor. 5:17).

The women's magazine *Missions Mosaic* followed Cathy for one year as she was transformed from caterpillar to butterfly. Each month, Cathy experienced the next step of her transformation. In the first article (September 1998), she was described as "newly hatched, content to eat and grow fuzzy." A year later, Cathy "has discovered that she was uniquely created, that she could soar above her old limitations. She has fulfilled the purpose for which she was made," (*Missions Mosaic*, August 1999). Transformation is God's work in your life. He makes you a new creature. Some caterpillars may be pretty, but no caterpillar knows true freedom and beauty apart from becoming a butterfly.

God wants you to know such freedom. His choice is that you soar. That is what transformation is all about. A friend of mine is going through a struggle right now that has her feeling trapped. The idea of soaring above the difficulties she is facing is hard for her to grasp, yet that is exactly the kind of transformation that God offers. Ask Jan Karon, author of the best-selling Mitford Series, how God transforms a life. At the age of 42, Karon (a divorced single mom without a high school education, at work in a successful but unfulfilling advertising career) asked Christ to come into her heart. A few years later, she risked all to follow God in a new career of writing. Since then, every book she has written allows readers an opportunity to hear and respond to the gospel of Christ.

How does God transform you? *He gives you a new nature.* A new inner voice guides your decisions and your attitudes. You find that your desires are changed. Your past attitudes toward things, people, time, world issues, government policies, home, family, and self are no longer satisfying. Even those things that you thought of as "must haves" for happiness are suddenly no longer necessary or even considered of value to you. You experience a new freedom as you discover that your possessions and desires no longer possess you.

He gives you a new goal. God's goal becomes your goal, a goal more magnificent and transcending than any personal goal you may have set before. Your new goal strengthens you to leap over the mud pits, to soar above the mountains, and to walk out of the dark valleys. Your goal is no longer to make it through this day. Your goal is no longer to survive a bad marriage or make a million bucks. You will find yourself saying to others, "I have never known such fulfillment, contentment, or excitement as I know now." Paul said, "Yes, we do have confidence, and we would rather be away from the body and at home with the Lord. So whether we are at home or away, we make it our aim to please [God]" (2 Cor. 5:8). Pleasing God becomes your goal.

He gives you a new motive. God's motive for you is His mercies in your life. "I appeal to you therefore, brothers and sisters, by the mercies of God" (Rom. 12:1). How great are God's mercies toward you? You cannot begin to list them. "I appeal to you therefore, brothers and sisters, by the mercies of God, to present your bodies as a living sacrifice, holy and acceptable to God, which is your spiritual worship" (Rom. 12:1). God's mercies make it possible for you to give yourself completely to Him. Who else to give your life, your possessions, your work, your family, your desires to than the God who has shown you such great mercies. No longer do you have to worry about who is going to come out on top, who will be the winner and who will be the loser. God's mercies as your motive free you to show the same mercies toward others. You do not have to push and pull to get your own way. You can enjoy living and giving and doing. The peace of right motive changes your home and your workplace. Your concern, in fact your joy, is to seek the best for others, to give up control, for now you know that all belongs to God and is in His control already. God is your motive.

❧ *God's Revolution*

"Then Elisha prayed: 'O Lord, please open his eyes that he may see.' So the Lord opened the eyes of the servant, and he saw; the mountain was full of horses and chariots of fire all around Elisha." (2 Kings 6:17)

A contemporary movie is based upon the true-life experience of a blind man who regained his sight for a brief time, only to lose it again. While he has his sight, he finds he is in a different world from the one he knew as a blind person. He is frightened and confused. He does not understand body language or simple everyday habits and actions that go with the seeing world. He is a captive of the blind culture.

From the moment of birth, whether we are blind or seeing, we are captives of our culture. We cannot see the world as a whole, without divisors, boundaries, and barriers. Only God has an unfettered view of the world. When we come to Him, communing with Him through prayer and Bible study, He revolutionizes our worldview. He allows us to see *His* culture, the only true and lasting culture. He *revolutionizes* our view of this life we live and the world in which we live it.

Regardless of how much we travel, how many experiences we have, how great our education, how many books we read or people we know or languages we speak, we are captives of our human culture apart from God. Simply, you and I are bound by a temporal understanding of the world around us. We describe one another with racial, political, national, educational, social, sexual, and religious language. Comprehension of truth, normal humanity, and real value are limited by our abnormal human- ness, our few experiences, our language, and our beliefs. Without God's eyesight we are blind to the very things God would choose for us to see and feel and be and do.

Theologians call this cultural understanding our "world- view." In fact, many theologians suggest that our worldview is reflective of our view of God. What lifestyle is the most God- like? How do we choose between what seems good and what is best in our world? What are the real issues regarding family, marriage, children, freedom, peace, hunger, ecology, govern- ing? What is our responsibility toward our neighbors? What is our relationship toward people of other genders, status levels, cultures, religions, and colors? Who do we really believe belongs in America? Or in our neighborhoods? Or next door? Does God really love all people?

When all of this is viewed through God's eyes, our percep- tion is revolutionized. We cannot keep from caring. We cannot keep from praying. We experience a true revolution in our think- ing and acting.

Extraordinary living depends on the correct worldview. Read Isaiah 42 for a glimpse of God's worldview. Who do you think is within the scope of God's love and redemption? Who is the servant given to nations? Who has been called and given as a covenant to the peoples? Who are the blind that God desires to lead on a new road? Who is God asking to "give heed" and "attend and listen" (verse 23)? Take time to let God speak to you and give you His answers to these questions.

ᴥ *God's Power*

"But you will receive power when the Holy Spirit has come upon you" (Acts 1:8).

The night that Hurricane Andrew came through Birmingham, Alabama, I saw flashes of blue shooting across the night sky all across the city. My husband and I went to the window to see this. We had never seen anything like it. Every few seconds another brilliant explosion of blue penetrated the darkness, showing the fury of the storm.

Later we learned that the blue came from transformers shorting out as the tremendous wind and rain tore into them. The city was left in darkness. The power needed to light our homes and keep us comfortable was gone. We experienced an unusually dark night.

Life's hurricanes are not the same as nature's hurricanes. Nature's forces may wipe out electrical power, but life's hurricanes cannot hinder God's power. God offers a power that is supernatural. He offers it every day of our lives, whether we are experiencing natural hurricanes or life hurricanes. Whatever our day holds, whether cleaning our homes, caring for sick children, driving car pools, teaching school, going on vacations, or working in stressful jobs, the same power that created the world is available to us for everyday living.

You may not have lived this day as though you have access to supernatural power. Most of us do not. For years, scientists have sought the secret to cold fusion, a source of power that is unlimited, clean, and safe. Some have come close to success, but they have not achieved their sought-after solution.

On the other hand, God's people have unlimited, supernatural power, and for the most part, they forget it even exists. We are so ready to give up when we hear the words *no, that can't be done, you're just a dreamer, there is no solution*, or *accept it*. Do any of these words sound familiar? Maybe you have said them, or they've been said to you.

Why would God choose to give us supernatural power if He knew we would do the ordinary or the expected with our lives and work and ministry? Doesn't it make sense that God's power is for something greater than this? What is it that God wants to do through you with *His* power? Forgive? Hope? Heal? Release the prisoner? Reach the world with the gospel? Grace to us all. We have the power of God to take on any challenge.

My life verse is Ephesians 3:20–21. Read it aloud with me: "Now to Him who by the power at work within us is able to accomplish abundantly far more than all we can ask or imagine, to Him be glory in the church and in Christ Jesus to all generations, forever and ever. Amen." The power is all yours.

❧ *God's Delight*

"Then I was beside him, like a master worker; and I was daily his delight, rejoicing before him always, rejoicing in his inhabited world and delighting in the human race" (Prov. 8:30–31).

Children delight in drawing close to their parents and grandparents. When I look through our photos, I find many snapshots of my grandchildren in their parents' lap or their grandparents' arms. Some Christian counselors suggest that we picture ourselves as children sitting in the lap of God with His arms around us, a way to feel safe and secure and to experience love and delight.

Delight is the natural outcome of drawing close to God. What better place to be than in the arms of the One who knows you best and loves you most? Could anything be more delightful than to hear the Creator of the universe call you, "My child"? Trust in the Father makes drawing close to God a life-changing experience. Jennifer Dean explains that the Hebrew word used for *delight* in Psalm 37:4 has its root in a word meaning "soft and pliable." Delight happens when the Father reaches out and draws you into His arms as you fold into His embrace, freely giving yourself to Him.

Your delight is also God's delight. He created you for fellowship with Him. He wants you to come to Him, draw close to Him, and call Him "Father." He wants intimate conversation, to share your daily walk, to meet your needs, to show you His plans, and to give you strength. He longs to make Himself known to you. He desires to transform your life so you can live abundantly. He longs to revolutionize your worldview so that you can join Him in the greatest adventure known to mankind. He has the power you need to live victoriously, to transform the world, to live extraordinarily!

❧ Resources for Extraordinary Living

Renee Baron and Elizabeth Wagele, *The Enneagram Made Easy*
(San Francisco: Harper, 1994).

Ron Boehme, *If God Has a Plan for My Life, Why Can't I Find It?*
(Seattle: YWAM, 1992).

Dietrich Bonhoeffer, *The Cost of Discipleship*
(New York: Collier, 1937).

Esther Burroughs, *A Garden Path to Mentoring*
(Birmingham: New Hope, 1997).

Stuart Calvert, *Uniquely Gifted*
(Birmingham: New Hope, 1993).

Danny Cox and John Hoover, *Seize the Day*
(Hawthorne, NJ: Career Press, 1994).

Jennifer Kennedy Dean, *Riches Stored in Secret Places*
(Birmingham: New Hope, 1996).

Jennifer Kennedy Dean, *Heart's Cry*
(Birmingham: New Hope, 1992).

Edna Ellison and Tricia Scribner, *Woman to Woman: Preparing Yourself to Mentor*
(Birmingham: New Hope Publishers, 1999).

Jerry D. Flack, *TalentEd: Strategies for Developing the Talent in Every Learner* (Englewood, CO: Teacher Ideas Press, 1993).

Richard Foster, *Freedom of Simplicity* (New York: Harper, 1981).

Richard Foster, *The Challenge of the Disciplined Life* (San Francisco: Harper, 1985).

Sarah Groves and Alicia Williamson, *A Seeking Heart: Rediscovering True Worship* (Birmingham: New Hope Publishers, 2000).

J. Grant Howard, *Balancing Life's Demands* (Sisters,OR: Multnomah, 1983).

Phillip Keller, *A Gardener Looks at Fruit of the Spirit* (Irving, TX: Word, 1986).

Rhonda Kelley, *A Woman's Guide to Personal Holiness* (Birmingham: New Hope, 2000).

Florence Littauer, *Personality Plus* (Grand Rapids: Fleming H. Revell, 1983).

Max Lucado, *God Came Near* (Sisters, OR: Multnomah, 1987).

Sally Magnusson, *The Flying Scotsman* (New York: Quartet Books, 1981).

Michael Michalko, *Thinkertoys: A Handbook of Business Creativity*
(Berkeley: Ten Speed Press, 1991).

Michael Michalko, *Thinkpak: A Brainstorming Card Deck*
(Berkeley: Ten Speed Press, 1994).

L. Jane Mohline, *A Woman of Excellence*
(Nashville: Broadman & Holman, 1991).

Andrea Mullins, Margaret Perkins, and Laura Savage,
*Gifted by God: Leading, Loving, and Teaching
with Your Life* Audio Cassette
(Birmingham: New Hope, 1997).

Robert W. Olson, *The Art of Creative Thinking*
(New York: HarperCollins, 1986).

Norman Vincent Peale, *The Power to Change Your Life*
(Pawling, NY: Foundation for Christian Living, 1972).

Tom Sine, *Mustard Seed Versus McWorld*
(Grand Rapids: Baker Books, 1999).

Bob Sjogren, *Unveiled at Last*
(Seattle: YWAM, 1992).

John Stott, *The Message of Ephesians*
(Downers Grove, IL: Intervarsity Press, 1979).

Reuben Welch, *We Really Do Need Each Other*
(Nashville: Generoux Nelson, 1973).

Sheila West, *Beyond Chaos: Stress Relief for the Working Woman*
(Colorado Springs: NavPress, 1991).

The New Bible Dictionary
(Grand Rapids: Eerdmans, 1962).

The Interpreter's Bible Vol. 11, *I and II Timothy and Titus*
(Nashville: Abingdon, 1955).

The Word in Life Study Bible
(Nashville: Thomas Nelson, 1993).